Zeng Zi Zi Si

THE GREAT LEARNING & THE DOCTRINE OF THE MEAN

曾子 子思 著

大学·中庸

〔英〕理雅各 翻译 杨文地 导读 注释

上海译文出版社

（一）学术经典提供思想源泉

两千六百年来的世界学术经典凝聚了人类思想的精华，世世代代的优秀思想家以他们独特的见识和智慧，留给后人取之不竭、用之不尽的思想源泉。从老子、孔子、柏拉图、亚里士多德以降，天才辈出，思想闪光，精彩纷呈。思想界的大师、名家们在人类思想史传统链条上的每一个环节，都启发后人开拓新的思想领域，探究生命的本质，直抵人性的深层。随着人类思想的不断成熟和完善，各个学科领域的理论从本体论、认识论、方法论、实践论、价值论等维度不断深化。后人继承前人的思想，借经典的滋养保持思想活力，丰富和发展前人的观点，使之形成一波又一波的思想洪流，从而改变人的思想和世界观，改变人类社会的进程。历史已经证明：人类社会的进步，思想的力量大于一切。

（二）学术经典传承精神力量

经典名著中蕴含的人类精神，传承的人类守望的共同价值原则和社会理想，在每一个具体领域里都有诸多丰富的表述，它们从整体上构成了推动人类进步的精神力量。研习和传承人类两千六百多年来的优秀思想，并将它化作求新求变的灵感，是人类文明的要义所在。仅有技术进步，还不足以表明人类的文明程度。若无优秀的思想底蕴，人类存在的意义将大打折扣。

中国思想传统中的基本理念和西方思想传统中的基本理念分别形成了东西方两大具有普遍价值的道德观念和价值系统。值得注意的是：(1) 这两大道德系统应该是一个互补、互鉴的整体，两

WAC

World Academic Classics
世界学术经典 · 英文版

总策划／总主编
庄智象　林骧华

上海时代教育出版研究中心 研发
Shanghai Epoch Education Publishing Research Center

世界学术经典（英文版）
总　序

书之成为经典，乃人类在不同时代的思想、智
晶，优秀文化之积淀，具有不随时代变易的永恒价
书须读经典，这是智者的共识。

对于中外经典著作中的思想表述，仅读外文书
言著作的白话释文是不够的，尤其是当误译、误
读者容易被误导，或望文生义，或以讹传讹，使
变成更深的文化隔阂。因此，在“世界学术经典（
目中，大部分作品为英文原著；原作是其他语种
相对可靠的英文译本；至于中国古代经典，则采
式呈现，旨在向西方阐释中国的思想和文化。其
经典是整个系列的重要组成部分。有了这一部分
体现出“世界性”。

以原典和英文方式出版，是为了使读者通过
以英文表达的思想、理论和方法，力求避免舛误，
和接受，化为智慧力量。这有利于思想的传播，
产生，同时亦可提高英语修养。

经典名著的重要性是不言而喻的，但是以下
再重申。

者都不可偏废，因为人类的思想是个多元整体。任何一个民族，缺少其中之一，在精神上都可能是不完整的；（2）这些基本理念都不是抽象概念，它们都具有很强的实践意义，并且必须由实践来考察，否则就很难体现其价值。

精神传承必然是一种自觉的过程，它靠习得，不靠遗传，因此我们需要研读经典。

（三）学术经典构成文化积淀

“文化”包含三大部分：（1）思想与精神现象；（2）制度与习俗；（3）有形的事物。学术经典是对思想与精神现象的归纳和提炼，对制度与习俗的探究和设计，对有形事物的形而上思考和描述。

每一个学科领域的经典著作中都会提出一些根本性的问题，这些问题直面人的困惑，思考人类社会的疑难，在新思想和新知识中展现人类的智慧。当这些思想成果积淀下来，就构成人类文化的主要组成部分。文化不只是制度或器物的外在形式，更重要的是凝结在其背后的精神与思想。

每一个学科的学术本身都要面对一些形而上的（超越性的、纯理论性的）文化问题。在很多人看来，理性的思考和理论的表述都是很枯燥的，但是热爱真理并且对思想情有独钟的人会从学术经典的理论中发现无限生动的天地，从而产生获得真理的快乐，这才是我们追求的真正文化。

大量阅读经典名著是一种学习、积累文化的根本方法，深度阅读和深刻记忆能使文化积淀在人的身上，并且代代相传。假如这一过程中断了，人世间只剩下花天酒地、歌舞升平，文化也就湮灭了。

（四）学术经典推动社会进步

毫无疑问，凡属学术经典，都必须含有新的学术成果——新思想、新理论、新方法，或者新探索。这样的原创性学术成果越多，人类的思想就越深邃，视野越开阔，理论更全面、完美，方法更先进、有效，社会的进步才能获得新的动力和保障。

人文主义推翻神学，理性主义旨在纠正人的偏激，启蒙精神主张打破思想束缚，多元主义反抗绝对理念。各种新思想层出不穷，带来了学术的进步，启发并推动了更大的社会变革。这些原创思想在历史长河中经过漫长的时间考验，成为经典，在任何一种文明中都是社会进步和发展的动力。

当我们研读完一部学术经典，分析和归纳其原创的思想观点时，可以很清晰地理解和感悟它在同时代的环境里对于社会的变革和进步有着何种意义，以及它对当下有哪些启迪。

相比技术的发展，思想并不浮显在社会的表层，它呈现在书本的字里行间，渗透于人的心智，在人的灵魂中闪光。每当社会需要时，它能让我们看到无形的巨大力量。

温故而知新。今日世界纷乱依旧，但时代已不再朦胧。人类思想史上的各种主张，在实践中都已呈现清晰的面貌。当我们重新梳理各种思想和理论时，自然不会再返回到“全盘接受”或者“全盘否定”的幼稚阶段。二十一世纪人类正确的世界观、人生观、价值观需要优秀思想传统的支撑，并通过批判继承，不断推陈出新，滋衍出磅礴之推力。

我们所选的这些学术经典，成书于不同的时代，代表了不同的思想与理论主张。有些著作带有时代烙印，有其局限性或片面性；有些观点不一定正确，但从另一个方面显示出人类思想的丰富性和复杂性。各门学科建立、各种主张提出之后，都曾经在历代思想的实验场上经受碰撞和检验，被接受或者被批判。我们的学者需要研读这些书，而青年学生们的思想成长更需要读这些书。当然，批评与分析是最有效和最有益的阅读方法。

有鉴于此，我们希望“世界学术经典（英文版）”能够真正做到“开卷有益”，使我们自己在潜移默化中都成长为有思想、有理想、有品位的人。

上海时代教育出版研究中心

2018 年 10 月

目录

《大学》导读
— 001 —

大　学
The Great Learning
— 005 —

经一章
— 006

传首章
— 010

传二章
— 012

传三章
— 014

传四章
— 018

传五章
— 020

传六章
— 022

传七章
— 024

传八章
— 026 —

传九章
— 028 —

传十章
— 034 —

《大学》术语汇编与简释
— 049 —

《中庸》导读
— 055 —

中 庸
The Doctrine of the Mean
— 061 —

第一章
— 062 —

第二章
— 066 —

第三章
— 068 —

第四章
— 070 —

第五章
— 072 —

第六章
— 074 —

第七章
— 076 —

第八章
— 078 —

第九章
— 080 —

第十章
— 082 —

第十一章
— 084 —

第十二章
— 086 —

第十三章
— 088 —

第十四章
— 092 —

第十五章
— 094 —

第十六章
— 096 —

第十七章
— 098 —

第十八章
— 100 —

第十九章
— 102 —

第二十章
— 106 —

第二十一章
— 120 —

第二十二章
— 122 —

第二十三章
— 124 —

第二十四章
— 126 —

第二十五章
— 128 —

第二十六章
— 130 —

第二十七章
— 134 —

第二十八章
— 136 —

第二十九章
— 138 —

第三十章
— 142 —

第三十一章
— 144 —

第三十二章
— 146 —

第三十三章
— 148 —

《中庸》术语汇编与简释
— 153 —

《大学》导读

杨文地

“四书”（《大学》《论语》《孟子》和《中庸》，这也是朱熹建议的阅读顺序）是中国科举制度时期教育的核心内容，十年寒窗苦读，为的就是一举成名。那么，人们能从“四书”中学到什么？从表面看，“四书”中详细描述规划了各种良好品行，如孝敬父母、尊敬长辈、诚实待人、关爱老幼、有错即改、谦虚谨慎、大公无私、以义为利不以利为利等等，但这还不是“四书”的核心关切。人们要问的是，究竟如何才能行为善事？如何才能成为“贤人”？如何才能发挥人们向善的能力？正是这些关切，才让朱熹耗尽一生，对《大学》《论语》《孟子》《中庸》进行了编撰和注释，使其成为一个完整的思想体系，探究了诸如人性、人心、人欲、人情、为学、格物等问题，阐释了人的品德状况和潜能。人之所以能够向善，关键在于人性本为善，而让本源的善发挥出来的途径就是修身。所以，“四书”中描述的修身过程为人们成贤成圣提供了可行路径。“人性本善”“人皆可圣贤”便成了“四书”体现的哲学思想。

《大学》原为《礼记》的第四十二篇，相传为春秋战国时期曾子（公元前505年—前435年）所作。宋代学者程颐认为，《大学》是儒学的入门读物。对《大学》和《中庸》的注释被称为

“章句”，而对《论语》和《孟子》的注释，因为引用了较多二程（程颐和程颢）及其弟子和他人的说法，则被称为“集注”，后人合称之为“四书章句集注”。朱熹认为，《大学》确立了儒学的基本规模和轮廓，因此将《大学》置于“四书”之首：“某要人先读大学，以定其规模；次读论语，以立其根本；次读孟子，以观其发越；次读中庸，以求古人之微妙（处）。大学一篇有等级次第，总作一处，易晓，宜先看。”朱熹在《大学》开篇之前引用子程子的话表达了同样的观点：“‘大学，孔氏之遗书。而初学入德之门也。’于今可见古人为学次第者，独赖此篇之存，而论、孟次之。学者必由是而学焉，则庶乎其不差矣。”

为了构筑“四书”的思想体系，朱熹将《大学》重新编辑，分为“经”和“传”两部分。“经”一章，“盖孔子之言，而曾子述之”；“传”十章，“曾子之意而门人记之也”，二者之间的关系是“以经统传，以传附经”。也就是说，“经”是基本观点，是纲领，“传”是对“经”的解释，附属于“经”。

“经”是指引人达到天下理想道德境界的重要篇章，分“三纲”（“明明德”“新民”和“止于至善”）和“八目”（“格物”“致知”“诚意”“正心”“修身”“齐家”“治国”“平天下”）。“三纲”之中，“明德”是“自然状态之本体”；“至善”是“通过人的努力，复其自然状态之本体”；“新民”是从“明德”到“至善”的桥梁。按照朱熹的解释，“自然状态之本体”就是“尽夫天理之极而无一毫人欲之私”的道德境界。“八目”的核心是“修身”，前四目是“修身”的方法，后三目是“修身”的目的。从“明德”到“至善”的整个过程需要通过“修身”来完成，所以《大学》突出强调的就是“自天子以至于庶人，壹是皆以修身为本”。

“传”十章的前四章是纲，论旨趣；后六章是目，体现功夫。根据朱熹的理解，“传”是对“经”的阐释，因此他对《大学》进行了重新编次，目的就是建构“传”与“经”的对应关系。例如，他以“克明德”“明命”“克明俊德”“皆自明也”解释“明明德”，以“日薪”“新民”“惟新”解释“新民”，以“止”“止于”解释“止于至善”。在重新编目之后，朱熹发现原文缺少“格物致知”的传文，这在他看来，“独其所谓格物致知者，字义不明，而传复阙焉，且为最初用力之地，而无复上文语绪之可寻也”。因此，朱熹认为有必要对格物致知进行重新阐释，弥补了该章，即第五章。特别需要说明的是，“传”的第十章内容深刻，重在阐述“治国平天下者，必须与民同好恶而不专其之利，通过亲、贤、乐、利各得其所，推进天下至太平”。“絜矩之道”是“平天下之要道”，是儒学的“以心度心、推己及人”思维方式的实际运用，而“国不以利为利，以义为利”代表了中国传统文化的核心理念和中华民族同世界交往所践行的实际原则。

《大学》所体现的儒家思想，千百年来一直影响着中国人，尽管有其历史局限性，但在当下仍有重要意义。《大学》三纲领之一的“明明德”，要求学习者弄清并彰显内心原有的光辉品德，向内感知自己的本真，从而达到精神醒悟。儒家思想强调“人之初，性本善”，而后天成长却产生好坏、善恶差异，其原因就是受社会环境的影响，因此社会环境与人性发展的关系是儒家教育考虑的重要方面。这些关系包括人与自我、人与他人、人与社会、人与世界。人生在世，不得不面对这四种关系，儒家面对这些关系，解决的良方就是“明明德”，通过教化、修身，洗涤原初本性的外在影响，彰显人性内在的光明美德。

三纲之二的“亲民”（又作“新民”），按程朱的阐释，就是“革其旧之谓也。言既自明其明德，又当推己及人，使之亦有以去其旧染之污也”。“明明德”是根据“大学之道”荡除自身之蒙，回归原初，而“亲民”更进一步要求人们在“明明德”基础之上，推己及人，帮助他人完成去除蒙昧而成为新人，这种“兼善”而非“独善”的教育思想正是大学教育的重要方面，也是知识共享的本质要求。如此一来，浑浊混沌的世界会越来越清洁美好。这也使儒家思想在当今以消费、竞争为主的世界大环境中成为一股清流。

但是，要成为清流谈何容易，其难点不在于自我启迪，而是要将其变成他人认可的思想并付诸行动。《大学》为此提供了出路，即三纲之三的“止于至善”。“止于至善”首先要“知止”，要知至善之地，知进退、悉厉害，有所为有所不为，去除杂念和私欲，不达人生完善之境绝不停息。这绝非一朝一夕可完成之事，要持之以恒、循序渐进、精益求精。

《大学》在指出大学之道三条纲领之后，明确了具体方法，即“八目”，强调心性之学，突出诚实、心诚、心正，让人见小利、大利而不为、不贪，至今仍具有现实意义。“八目”前五目是“内圣”之学，强调自我修养，后三目为“外王”，强调在完善自我修养的基础上才有可能“齐家”“治国”“平天下”。当然，二者并非必然联系，后者的达成还受其他因素（如制度）的影响，但“内圣”始终是根本。学习《大学》的关键就是要结合当下，汲取其有生命力之处，剔除其僵化过时的地方，推陈出新，追寻本质而美好的原初所在。

大　学

The Great Learning[1]

1. The Great Learning: 理雅各（James Legge）认为“大学”应该按字面译为“The Great Learning”，尽管郑玄和朱熹对此解释有分歧。郑玄认为“大”解释同“太”，“大学，以其记博学，可以为政”；孔颖达也持有类似见解，“大学，至道矣”。但朱熹认为“大学者，大人之学也”。理雅各遵循中国古书使用开篇两个字作为标题的传统，按字面意义将其译为“The Great Learning”。但是，根据朱熹的解释以及具体内容，陈荣捷（Wing-tsit Chan）的翻译“The Way of Learning to be Great”或浦安迪（Andrew H. Plaks）的翻译“Ta Hsüeh (The Highest Order of Cultivation)”也许更为贴切。

经一章

大学[1]之道，在明[2]明德[3]，在亲[4]民，在止于至善[5]。知止[6]而后有定[7]，定而后能静[8]，静而后能安[9]，安而后能虑[10]，虑而后能得。物有本末[11]，事有终始[12]，知所先后，则近道矣。

---

1. 大学：成人之学，成人的教育。
2. 明：彰显。
3. 明德：光明美好的德性，指人善良的本性。
4. 亲：当作"新"，革新。
5. 至善：事理当然之极，极致。
6. 止：当停之处，指事理极致之处。
7. 定：确定的目标。
8. 静：心不妄动，内心平静。
9. 安：安于所处。
10. 虑：处事精详，思虑周全。
11. 本末：主要和次要之分。此处明德为本，新民为末。
12. 终始：知止为始，能得为终。

1. What the Great Learning teaches, is — to illustrate[1] illustrious virtue; to renovate[2] the people; and to rest in the highest excellence[3].

2. The point where to rest being known, the object of pursuit is then determined; and, that being determined, a calm unperturbedness may be attained. To that calmness there will succeed a tranquil repose. In that repose there may be careful deliberation, and that deliberation will be followed by the attainment of the desired end.

3. Things have their root and their branches. Affairs have their end and their beginning. To know what is first and what is last will lead near to what is taught in *the Great Learning*.

---

1. illustrate: 该词的原始含义为“照亮，阐明”，引申为“彰显”。同理，“illustrious”意为“清楚的，明亮的”，引申为“光明美好的”。
2. renovate：有些译本将“亲”译为“love”。根据文内阐释，此处“亲”当作“新”，为“革新”之意，因此译为“renovate”。
3. the highest excellence：“excellence”本身已经具有最高级含义，再加上“highest”来修饰，不符合英文表达习惯，体现出理雅各尽力忠实原文的翻译原则。“止于至善”是指极致的获得后的停息，“至善”隐藏了“获得”这个动作，综合浦安迪的翻译“the fullest attainment of the good”，不妨译为“the fullest attainment of excellence”。

古之欲明明德于天下者，先治其国；欲治其国者，先齐其家；欲齐其家者，先修其身；欲修其身者，先正其心；欲正其心者，先诚其意；欲诚其意者，先致其知；致知在格物。物格而后知至，知至而后意诚，意诚而后心正，心正而后身修，身修而后家齐，家齐而后国治，国治而后天下平。自天子以至于庶人，壹是[1]皆以修身为本。其本乱而末治者否矣，其所厚者薄，而其所薄者厚，未之有也！

---

1. 壹是：一切，一律。

4. The ancients who wished to illustrate illustrious virtue throughout the empire, first ordered well their own States. Wishing to order well their States, they first regulated their families. Wishing to regulate their families, they first cultivated their persons. Wishing to cultivate their persons, they first rectified their hearts. Wishing to rectify their hearts, they first sought to be sincere in their thoughts. Wishing to be sincere in their thoughts, they first extended to the utmost their knowledge. Such extension of knowledge lay in the investigation of things.

5. Things being investigated, knowledge became complete.[1] Their knowledge being complete, their thoughts were sincere. Their thoughts being sincere, their hearts were then rectified. Their hearts being rectified, their persons were cultivated. Their persons being cultivated, their families were regulated. Their families being regulated, their States were rightly governed. Their States being rightly governed, the whole empire was made tranquil and happy.

6. From the emperor down to the mass of the people, all must consider the cultivation of the person the root of every thing besides.

7. It cannot be, when the root is neglected, that what should spring from it will be well ordered. It never has been the case that what was of great importance has been slightly cared for, and, at the same time, that what was of slight importance has been greatly cared for.

---

1. Things being investigated, knowledge became complete：原文表达的逻辑关系是必要条件，“物格才有可能知至”，而译文变成充分条件，“只要物格就可以知至”，犯了逻辑错误。以下直到“Their States being rightly governed, the whole empire was made tranquil and happy”都有类似逻辑错误。

传首章

康诰[1]曰:"克[2]明德。"大甲[3]曰:"顾[4]諟[5]天之明命。"帝典[6]曰:"克明峻[7]德。"皆自明也。

1. 康诰:《尚书·周书》中的一篇。
2. 克:能够。
3. 大甲:《尚书·商书》中的一篇。
4. 顾:顾念。
5. 諟(shì):古字,同"是",这个。
6. 帝典:即《尧典》,《尚书·虞书》中的一篇。
7. 峻:大,高尚。

1. In the Announcement to Kang, it is said, “He was able to make his virtue illustrious.”

2. In the Tai Jia, it is said, “He contemplated and studied the illustrious decrees of Heaven[1].”

3. In the Canon of the Emperor Yao, it is said, “He was able to make illustrious his lofty virtue.”

4. These passages all show how those sovereigns made themselves illustrious.

---

1. Heaven：“天”译为“Heaven”，具有了宗教含义，而中国的“天”指最高的主宰，是个终极概念，代表了“至高无上”，不具有具象性。而“Tian”体现了中国特有的概念，同时兼顾读者的理解，因此，作为抽象符号，直译为“Tian”更好。

传二章

汤[1]之盘[2]铭曰："苟[3]日新，日日新，又日新。"康诰曰："作[4]新民。"诗[5]曰："周虽旧邦，其命[6]惟新。"是故君子无所不用其极。

1. 汤：商朝开国君主成汤。
2. 盘：沐浴用的器具。
3. 苟：如果。
4. 作：鼓舞，振作。
5. 诗：《诗经·大雅·文王》。
6. 命：禀受的天命。

1. On the bathing-tub of Tang, the following words were engraved: — "If you can one day renovate yourself, do so from day to day. Yea, let there be daily renovation."

2. In the Announcement to Kang, it is said, "To stir up the new people[1]."

3. In the Book of Poetry, it is said, "Although Chow (Zhou)[2] was an ancient state, the ordinance which lighted on it was new."

4. Therefore, the superior man in everything uses his utmost endeavours.

---

1. To stir up the new people：原句意为"鼓励人们自新"，译文回译是"煽动新人"，可改译为"to encourage people to renovate themselves"。
2. Chow (Zhou)：周朝。为方便读者，书中所涉拼音处全部采用现代汉语拼音。

传三章

诗[1]云："邦畿[2]千里，惟民所止[3]。"诗[4]云："缗蛮[5]黄鸟，止于丘隅[6]。"子曰："于止，知其所止，可以人而不如鸟乎！"诗[7]云："穆穆[8]文王，於[9]缉[10]熙[11]敬止！"为人君，止于仁；为人臣，止于敬；为人子，止于孝；为人父，止于慈；与国人交，止于信。

---

1. 诗：《诗经·商颂·玄鸟》。
2. 邦畿（jī）：天子所在的都城。
3. 止：居住的地方。
4. 诗：《诗经·小雅·绵蛮》。
5. 缗（mín）蛮：鸟叫声。
6. 丘隅：草木茂盛的地方。
7. 诗：《诗经·大雅·文王》。
8. 穆穆：深远的样子。形容文王仪表端庄、行止恭敬。
9. 於（wū）：叹美词。
10. 缉：继续。
11. 熙：光明。

1. In the Book of Poetry, it is said, "The imperial domain of a thousand *li* is where the people rest."

2. In the Book of Poetry, it is said, "The twittering yellow bird rests on a corner of the mound[1]." The Master said, "When it rests, it knows where to rest. Is it possible that a man should not be equal to this bird?"

3. In the Book of Poetry, it is said, "Profound was King Wen. With how bright and unceasing a feeling of reverence did he regard his resting places!" As a sovereign, he rested in benevolence[2]. As a minister, he rested in reverence. As a son, he rested in filial piety. As a father, he rested in kindness. In communication with his subjects, he rested in good faith.

---

1. a corner of the mound：理雅各对"丘隅"的翻译"a corner of the mound"与原文含义不符，可采用陈荣捷的译文"a thickly wooded mount"。
2. benevolence："仁"译为"benevolence"具有宗教意义，同时也缩小了"仁"的意义，可以音译为"Ren"，或者采用浦安迪的翻译"human kindness"。

诗[1]云："瞻彼淇澳[2]，菉[3]竹猗猗[4]。有斐[5]君子，如切如磋，如琢如磨。瑟[6]兮僩[7]兮，赫兮喧兮。有斐君子，终不可諠[8]兮！"如切如磋者，道学也；如琢如磨者，自修也；瑟兮僩兮者，恂栗[9]也；赫兮喧兮者，威仪也；有斐君子，终不可諠兮者，道盛德至善，民之不能忘也。诗[10]云："於戏[11]前王不忘！"君子贤其贤而亲其亲，小人乐其乐而利其利，此以没世不忘也。

---

1. 诗：《诗经·卫风·淇澳》。
2. 澳（yù）：弯弯曲曲的岸边。
3. 菉（lù）：通"绿"。
4. 猗猗（yī）：美好盛大的样子。
5. 斐：文质彬彬的样子。
6. 瑟：严密，严谨。
7. 僩（xiàn）：威武的样子。
8. 諠（xuān）：忘记。
9. 恂（xún）栗：恐惧战栗。
10. 诗：《诗经·周颂·烈文》。
11. 於戏（wūhū）：叹词，同"呜呼"。

4. In the Book of Poetry, it is said, "Look at that winding course of the (river) *Qi*, with the green bamboos so luxuriant! Here is our elegant and accomplished prince[1]! As we cut and then file; as we chisel and then grind: so has he cultivated himself. How grave is he and dignified! How majestic and distinguished! Our elegant and accomplished prince never can be forgotten." That expression — "as we cut and then file," indicates the work of learning. "As we chisel, and then grind," indicates that of self-culture. "How grave is he and dignified!" indicates the feeling of cautious reverence. "How majestic and distinguished!" indicates an awe-inspiring deportment[2]. "Our elegant and accomplished prince never can be forgotten," indicates how, when virtue is complete and excellence extreme, the people cannot forget them.

5. In the Book of Poetry, it is said, "Ah! the former kings are not forgotten." Future princes[3] deem worthy what they deemed worthy, and love what they loved. The common people delight in what they delighted, and are benefited by their beneficial arrangements. It is on this account that the former kings, after they have quitted the world, are not forgotten.

---

1. prince："君子"按字面译为"prince"有失原意，此处"君子"可泛指"德才出众之人"，不妨译为"gentleman"。
2. deportment：指人的风度仪态。
3. princes：此处"君子"与"前王"相对，可泛指后王，即统治者，因此此处"君子"不妨译为"kings"或者"rulers"。

传四章

子曰:“听讼[1],吾犹人[2]也,必也使无讼乎!”无情者[3]不得尽其辞，大畏[4]民志[5]，此谓知本[6]。

1. 听讼：审理案件。讼：争辩是非。
2. 犹人：和别人一样。
3. 无情者：隐瞒实情的人。
4. 畏：使……畏服。
5. 民志：民心。
6. 知本：知道本末先后的次序。

The Master said, "In hearing litigations, I am like any other body. What is necessary is to cause the people to have no litigations." So, those who are devoid of principle[1] find it impossible to carry out their speeches, and a great awe would be struck into men's minds; — this is called knowing the root[2].

1. devoid of principle：直译为"没有原则的人"，与原文"无情者"（指隐瞒实情的人）含义不符，不妨采用陈荣捷的翻译"those who would not tell the truth"。
2. knowing the root：此处"知本"具体指"无情者不得尽其言，大畏民志"，这才是问题的根本所在。不妨改译为"knowing the root, or the fundamentals"。

传五章

此谓知本。[1]（所谓致知在格物者，言欲致吾之知，在即物而穷其理也。盖人心之灵莫不有知，而天下之物莫不有理，惟于理有未穷，故其知有不尽也。是以大学始教，必使学者即凡天下之物，莫不因其已知之理而益穷之，以求至乎其极。至于用力之久，而一旦豁然贯通焉，则众物之表里精粗无不到，而吾心之全体大用无不明矣。此谓物格，）[2]此谓知之至也。

1. 此谓知本：程颐与朱熹都认为此句为衍文，应删。
2. 所谓致知在格物者……此谓物格：按照朱熹的注释，本章应阐释“格物致知之义”，但缺少相应内容，于是朱熹根据程颐之意作了补传将其完善。

1. This is called knowing the root, or the fundamentals.

(2. The meaning of the expression, "The perfecting of knowledge depends on the investigation of things," is this: — If we wish to carry our knowledge to the utmost, we must investigate the principles of all things we come into contact with, for the intelligent mind of man is certainly formed to know, and there is not a single thing in which its principles do not inhere. But so long as all principles are not investigated, man's knowledge is incomplete.

3. On this account, the Great Learning for adults, at the outset of its lessons, instructs the learner, in regard to all things in the world, to proceed from what knowledge he has of their principles, and pursue his investigation of them, till he reaches the extreme point.

4. After exerting himself in this way for a long time, he will suddenly find himself possessed of a wide and far-reaching penetration. Then, the qualities of all things, whether external or internal, the subtle or the coarse, will all be apprehended, and the mind, in its entire substance and its relations to things, will be perfectly intelligent.

5. This is called the investigation of things.)

6. This is called the perfection of knowledge.

传六章

所谓诚其意[1]者，毋自欺也，如恶[2]恶臭，如好[3]好色，此之谓自谦[4]，故君子必慎[5]其独也！小人闲居[6]为不善，无所不至，见君子而后厌然[7]，掩其不善，而著其善。人之视己，如见其肺肝然，则何益矣。此谓诚于中，形于外，故君子必慎其独也。曾子曰："十目所视，十手所指，其[8]严乎！"富润屋，德润身，心广体胖[9]，故君子必诚其意。

---

1. 诚其意：使意念真诚。
2. 恶：讨厌。
3. 好：喜欢。
4. 谦：通"慊"（qiè），满足，满意。
5. 慎：谨慎。
6. 闲居：独处。
7. 厌然：沮丧、躲闪。
8. 其（qǐ）：同"岂"，难道不是。
9. 胖（pán）：安闲舒适。

1. What is meant by "making the thoughts sincere," is the allowing no self-deception, as when we hate a bad smell, and as when we love what is beautiful. This is called self-enjoyment. Therefore, the superior man must be watchful over himself when he is alone[1].

2. There is no evil to which the mean man, dwelling retired, will not proceed, but when he sees a superior man, he instantly tries to disguise himself, concealing his evil, and displaying what is good. The other beholds him, as if he saw his heart and veins; — of what use is his disguise? This is an instance of the saying — "What truly is within will be manifested without[2]." Therefore, the superior man must be watchful over himself when he is alone.

3. The disciple Zeng said, "What ten eyes behold, what ten hands point to, is to be regarded with reverence[3]!"

4. Riches adorn a house, and virtue adorns the person. The mind is expanded, and the body is at ease. Therefore, the superior man must make his thoughts sincere.

---

1. when he is alone：“独”的理解和翻译存在歧义，一解指“内心”，一解指“独处”。理雅各选择了第二种解释，但根据上下文以及相关文献对“独”的阐释，第一种解释更全面，包含“独处”之意。所以，“独”不妨译作“his secret thoughts”“his secret self”，或者“his inner self”。
2. without：〈古或诗／文〉在外面，在外部。
3. with reverence：此处指内在的善与恶是无法掩饰的，需令人畏惧，因此可改译为“With ten eyes beholding and ten hands pointing to, isn't that aweful?”

传七章

所谓修身在正其心者，身有所忿懥[1]，则不得其正；有所恐惧，则不得其正；有所好乐，则不得其正；有所忧患，则不得其正。心不在焉，视而不见，听而不闻，食而不知其味。此谓修身在正其心。

---

1. 忿懥（zhì）：愤怒的样子。

1. What is meant by "The cultivation of the person depends on rectifying the mind," may be thus illustrated: — If a man be under the influence of passion, he will be incorrect in his conduct. He will be the same, if he is under the influence of terror, or under the influence of fond regard, or under that of sorrow and distress.

2. When the mind is not present, we look and do not see; we hear and do not understand; we eat and do not know the taste of what we eat.

3. This is what is meant by saying that the cultivation of the person depends on the rectifying of the mind.

传八章

所谓齐其家在修其身者，人之其所亲爱而辟[1]焉，之其所贱恶而辟焉，之其所畏敬而辟焉，之其所哀矜[2]而辟焉，之其所敖[3]惰[4]而辟焉。故好而知其恶，恶而知其美者，天下鲜矣！故谚有之曰："人莫知其子之恶，莫知其苗之硕。"此谓身不修不可以齐其家。

1. 辟（pì）：同"僻"，偏颇。
2. 哀矜：哀怜，怜悯。
3. 敖：通"傲"，傲慢自大。
4. 惰：怠慢轻视。

1. What is meant by "The regulation of one's family depends on the cultivation of his person," is this: — Men are partial where they feel affection and love; partial where they despise and dislike; partial where they stand in awe and reverence; partial where they feel sorrow and compassion; partial where they are arrogant and rude. Thus it is that there are few men in the world, who love, and at the same time know the bad qualities of the object of their love, or who hate, and yet know the excellences of the object of their hatred.

2. Hence it is said, in the common adage, "A man does not know the wickedness of his son; he does not know the richness of his growing corn."

3. This is what is meant by saying that if the person be not cultivated, a man cannot regulate his family.

传九章

所谓治国必先齐其家者，其家不可教而能教人者，无之。故君子不出家而成教于国：孝者，所以事君也；弟[1]者，所以事长也；慈[2]者，所以使众也。康诰曰“如保赤子”，心诚求之，虽不中，不远矣。未有学养子而后嫁者也！一家[3]仁，一国兴仁；一家让，一国兴让；一人贪戾，一国作乱；其机[4]如此。此谓一言偾[5]事，一人定国。

---

1. 弟（tì）：同“悌”，敬爱兄长。
2. 慈：疼爱子女。
3. 家：此处指国君一家，但在当下可泛指普通人家，这才具有“国家兴亡，匹夫有责”的现实意义。
4. 机：关联，缘由。
5. 偾（fèn）：颠覆，败坏。

1. What is meant by "In order rightly to govern his State, it is necessary first to regulate his family," is this: — It is not possible for one to teach others, while he cannot teach his own family. Therefore, the ruler, without going beyond his family, completes the lessons for the State. There is filial piety: — therewith the sovereign should be served. There is fraternal submission: — therewith elders and superiors should be served. There is kindness: — therewith the multitude should be treated.

2. In the Announcement to Kang, it is said, "Act as if you were watching over an infant." If a mother is really anxious about it, though she may not hit exactly the wants of her infant, she will not be far from doing so. There never has been a girl who learned to bring up a child, that she might afterwards marry.

3. From the loving example of one family of the ruler, a whole State becomes loving, and from its courtesies, the whole State becomes courteous, while, from the ambition and perverseness of the one man or the ruler, the whole State may be led to rebellious disorder; — such is the nature of the influence. This verifies the saying, "Affairs may be ruined by a single sentence; a kingdom may be settled by its ruler."

尧舜帅[1]天下以仁，而民从[2]之；桀纣帅天下以暴，而民从之；其所令反其所好，而民不从。是故君子有诸己而后求[3]诸人，无诸己而后非诸人。所藏乎身不恕[4]，而能喻[5]诸人者，未之有也。故治国在齐其家。

---

1. 帅：同“率”，率领。
2. 从：跟从，跟随。
3. 求：要求。
4. 恕：推己及人。
5. 喻：晓喻，告知。

4. Yao and Shun led on the empire with benevolence, and the people followed them. Këë (Jie) and Chow (Zhou) led on the empire with violence, and the people followed them. The orders which these issued were contrary to the practices which they loved, and so the people did not follow them. On this account, the ruler must himself be possessed of the good qualities, and then he may require them in the people. He must not have the bad qualities in himself, and then he may require that they shall not be in the people. Never has there been a man, who, not having reference to his own character and wishes in dealing with others, was able effectually to instruct them.

5. Thus we see how the government of the State depends on the regulation of the family.

诗[1]云："桃之夭夭[2]，其叶蓁蓁[3]；之子[4]于归[5]，宜[6]其家人。"宜其家人，而后可以教国人。诗[7]云："宜兄宜弟。"宜兄宜弟，而后可以教国人。诗[8]云："其仪[9]不忒[10]，正是[11]四国。"其为父子兄弟足[12]法[13]，而后民法之也。此谓治国在齐其家。

---

1. 诗：《诗经·周南·桃夭》。
2. 夭夭（yāo）：鲜美嫩弱的样子。
3. 蓁蓁（zhēn）：草木茂盛的样子。
4. 之子：这个女子。
5. 于归：出嫁。
6. 宜：善，使和顺美满。
7. 诗：《诗经·小雅·蓼萧》。
8. 诗：《诗经·曹风·鸤鸠》。
9. 仪：仪表。
10. 忒：差错。
11. 正是：成为表率。
12. 足：值得。
13. 法：效法。

6. In the Book of Poetry, it is said, "That peach tree, so delicate and elegant! How luxuriant is its foliage! This girl is going to get married. She will rightly order her household." Let the household be rightly ordered, and then the people of the State may be taught.[1]

7. In the Book of Poetry, it is said, "They can discharge their duties to their elder brothers. They can discharge their duties to their younger brothers." Let the ruler discharge his duties to his elder and younger brothers, and then he may teach the people of the State.[2]

8. In the Book of Poetry, it is said, "In his deportment there is nothing wrong; he rectifies all the people of the State." Yes; when the ruler, as a father, a son, and a brother, is a model, then the people imitate him.

9. This is what is meant by saying, "The government of his kingdom depends on his regulation of the family."

---

1. She will rightly ... the State may be taught：与原文有出入，采用 Andrew Plaks 的译文："She will surely bring goodness to all the members of her new household." Only when one brings goodness to the members of one's household is one in a position to provide moral instruction to all the people of the State.
2. They can discharge ... teach the people of the State：与原文有出入，采用 Andrew Plaks 的译文："He brings goodness to his brothers, elder and younger alike." Only when one brings goodness to his brothers is one in a position to provide moral instruction to all the people of the State.

传十章

所谓平天下在治其国者，上老老[1]而民兴孝，上长长[2]而民兴弟，上恤孤而民不倍[3]，是以君子有絜矩[4]之道也。所恶[5]于上，毋以使下；所恶于下，毋以事上；所恶于前，毋以先后；所恶于后，毋以从前；所恶于右，毋以交于左；所恶于左，毋以交于右：此之谓絜矩之道。

---

1. 老老：孝敬长辈。
2. 长长：尊敬兄长。
3. 倍：通“背”，背弃。
4. 絜矩（xiéjǔ）：法度。絜，度量；矩，画方形或直角的用具。絜矩之道指君子的言行要有示范作用，使上下四旁均齐方正。
5. 恶：厌恶。

1. What is meant by "The making the whole empire peaceful and happy depends on the government of his State," is this: — When the sovereign behaves to his aged, as the aged should be behaved to, the people become filial; when the sovereign behaves to his elders, as elders should be behaved to, the people learn brotherly submission; when the sovereign treats compassionately the young and helpless, the people do the same. Thus the ruler has a principle with which, as with a measuring square, may regulate his conduct.[1]

2. What a man dislikes in his superiors, let him not display in the treatment of his inferiors; what he dislikes in his inferiors, let him not display in the service of his superiors; what he hates in those who are before him, let him not therewith precede those who are behind him; what he hates in those who are behind him, let him not therewith follow those who are before him; what he hates to receive on the right, let him not bestow on the left; what he hates to receive on the left, let him not bestow on the right: — this is what is called "The principle, with which, as with a measuring square, to regulate one's conduct." [2]

---

1. Thus the ruler ... may regulate his conduct：与原文有出入，可改译为 "Thus the ruler has a principle with which, as with a measuring square, may regulate his conduct and make himself an exemplar for others"。
2. The principle ... to regulate one's conduct：同上，增加 "and make oneself an exemplar for others"。

诗[1]云："乐[2]只[3]君子，民之父母。"民之所好好之，民之所恶恶之，此之谓民之父母。诗[4]云："节[5]彼南山，维石岩岩[6]，赫赫师尹[7]，民具尔瞻。"有国者不可以不慎，辟[8]则为天下僇[9]矣。诗[10]云："殷之未丧师[11]，克配上帝；仪[12]监[13]于殷，峻[14]命不易[15]。"道得众则得国，失众则失国。

1. 诗：《诗经・小雅・南山有台》。
2. 乐：快乐，和美。
3. 只：语气助词。
4. 诗：《诗经・小雅・节南山》。
5. 节：截然高大的样子。
6. 岩岩：高耸。
7. 师尹：周太师尹氏。
8. 辟：偏。
9. 僇：通"戮"，杀戮。
10. 诗：《诗经・大雅・文王》。
11. 师：民众。
12. 仪：宜。
13. 监：鉴。
14. 峻：大。
15. 不易：难以保守。

3. In the Book of Poetry, it is said, "How much to be rejoiced in are these princes[1], the parents of the people!" When a prince loves what the people love, and hates what the people hate, then is he what is called the parent of the people.

4. In the Book of Poetry, it is said, "Lofty is that southern hill, with its rugged masses of rocks! Greatly distinguished are you, O Marshal Yin, the people all look up to you." Rulers of kingdoms may not neglect to be careful. If they deviate to a mean selfishness, they will be a disgrace in the empire.

5. In the Book of Poetry, it is said, "Before the sovereigns of the Yin Dynasty had lost the hearts of the people, they could stand as equals before Heaven. Take warning from the house of Yin. The great decree is not easily preserved." This shows that, by gaining the people, the kingdom is gained, and, by losing the people, the kingdom is lost.

---

1. princes：《大学》经常引用《诗经》，其中同一个词往往会有不同的含义。《诗经·小雅·南山有台》"乐只君子"中的"君子"，即被祝寿的主人。其身体健康、精神矍铄、德行优良、深受人们敬爱，但具体身份不明，可以是德高望重的贵族，也可以理解为君子贤人。而引文之外下一句"民之所好好之，民之所恶恶之，此之谓民之父母"中隐含的主语"君子"则指统治者。所以，引用《诗经》时，"君子"可译为"gentleman"，其他译为"ruler"或者"King"。

是故君子先慎乎德。有德此有人，有人此有土，有土此有财，有财此有用。德者本也，财者末也，外本内末，争民施夺。是故财聚则民散，财散则民聚。是故言悖而出者，亦悖而入；货悖而入者，亦悖而出。

6. On this account, the ruler will first take pains about his own virtue. Possessing virtue will give him the people. Possessing the people will give him the territory. Possessing the territory will give him its wealth. Possessing the wealth, he will have resources for expenditure.

7. Virtue is the root; wealth is the result.

8. If he make the root his secondary object, and the result his primary, he will only wrangle with his people, and teach them rapine.

9. Hence, the accumulation of wealth is the way to scatter the people; and the letting it be scattered among them is the way to collect the people.

10. And hence, the ruler's words going forth contrary to right, will come back to him in the same way, and wealth, gotten by improper ways, will take its departure by the same.

康诰曰："惟命[1]不于常[2]！"道[3]善则得之，不善则失之矣。楚书曰："楚国无以为宝，惟善以为宝。"舅犯[4]曰："亡人[5]无以为宝，仁亲以为宝。"秦誓[6]曰："若有一个臣，断断[7]兮无他技，其心休休[8]焉，其如有容焉。人之有技，若己有之，人之彦[9]圣[10]，其心好之，不啻[11]若自其口出，寔[12]能容之，以能保我子孙黎民，尚亦有利哉。人之有技，媢[13]疾以恶之，人之彦圣，而违[14]之俾[15]不通，寔不能容，以不能保我子孙黎民，亦曰殆哉。"

---

1. 命：天命。
2. 常：固定不变的。
3. 道：言。
4. 舅犯：晋文公重耳的舅舅狐偃，字子犯。
5. 亡人：流亡的人，此处指重耳，其为公子时曾在外流亡十九年。
6. 秦誓：《尚书·周书》中的一篇。
7. 断断：心志专一。
8. 休休：心胸开阔。
9. 彦：俊美。
10. 圣：通明。
11. 不啻（chì）：不止，不只。
12. 寔（shí）：通"实"，确实。
13. 媢（mào）：嫉妒。
14. 违：违逆，阻碍。
15. 俾（bǐ）：使，把。

11. In the Announcement to Kang, it is said, "The decree indeed may not always rest on us;" that is, goodness obtains the decree, and the want of goodness loses it.

12. In the Book of Chu, it is said, "The kingdom of Chu does not consider that[1] to be valuable. It values, instead, its good men."

13. Duke Wen's uncle, Fan, said, "Our fugitive does not account that[2] to be precious. What he considers precious, is the affection due to his parent."

14. In the Declaration of the duke of Qin, it is said, "Let me have but one minister, plain and sincere, not pretending to other abilities, but with a simple, upright, mind; and possessed of generosity, regarding the talents of others as though he himself possessed them, and, where he finds accomplished and perspicacious men, loving them in his heart more than his mouth expresses, and really showing himself able to bear them and employ them: — such a minister will be able to preserve my sons and grandsons, and black-haired people[3], and benefits likewise to the kingdom may well be looked for from him. But if it be his character, when he finds men of ability, to be jealous and hate them; and, when he finds accomplished and perspicacious[4] men, to oppose them and not allow their advancement, showing himself really not able to bear them: — such a minister will not be able to protect my sons and grandsons and black-haired people; and may he not also be pronounced dangerous to the State?"

---

1. that：指财富。
2. that：同上。
3. black-haired people：common people，黎民。
4. perspicacious：敏锐的，有洞察力的。

唯仁人放流之，迸[1]诸四夷，不与同中国。此谓唯仁人为能爱人，能恶人。见贤而不能举，举而不能先，命[2]也；见不善而不能退，退而不能远，过也。好人之所恶，恶人之所好，是谓拂[3]人之性，菑[4]必逮[5]夫身。是故君子有大道，必忠信以得之，骄泰[6]以失之。

1. 迸：同“屏”，驱逐。
2. 命：根据郑玄的注释，“命”应为“慢”，意为怠慢，轻慢。
3. 拂：违背。
4. 菑（zāi）：同“灾”。
5. 逮：达到。
6. 骄泰：骄傲自大，奢侈放纵。

15. It is only the truly virtuous man, who can send away such a man and banish him, driving him out among the barbarous tribes around, determined not to dwell along with him in the Middle kingdom. This is in accordance with the saying, "It is only the truly virtuous man who can love or who can hate others."

16. To see men of worth and not be able to raise them to office; to raise them to office, but not to do so quickly: — this is disrespect[1]. To see bad men and not be able to remove them; to remove them, but not to do so to a distance: — this is weakness[2].

17. To love those whom men hate, and to hate those whom men love: — this is to outrage the natural feeling of men. Calamities cannot fail to come down on him who does so.

18. Thus we see that the sovereign has a great course to pursue. He must show entire self-devotion and sincerity to attain it, and by pride and extravagance he will fail of it.

---

1. disrespect：根据郑玄的注释，"命"应作"慢"，所以译为"disrespect"，表示"轻慢"。
2. weakness：理雅各对"过"的翻译仍然是根据语境的灵活处理，指缺乏决断，做事不够果敢，这是骄恣放纵的结果，与下文的"骄泰"意义更融洽。

生财有大道，生之者众[1]，食之者寡[2]，为之者疾[3]，用之者舒[4]，则财恒足矣。仁者以财发[5]身，不仁者以身发财。未有上好仁而下不好义者也，未有好义其事不终者也，未有府库财非其财者也。

---

1. 生之者众：国境之内游手好闲的民众少了则财物的创造者就多了。
2. 食之者寡：朝堂上尸位素餐的官员少了则财物的消耗者就少了。
3. 为之者疾：不占用农耕时节则民众生产财物的速度就会加快。
4. 用之者舒：根据收入来决定开支则消费财物时就懂得节俭。
5. 发：提高，发达。

19. There is a great course also for the production of wealth. Let the producers be many and the consumers few. Let there be activity in the production, and economy in the expenditure. Then the wealth will always be sufficient.

20. The virtuous ruler, by means of his wealth, makes himself more distinguished. The vicious ruler accumulates wealth, at the expense of his life.

21. Never has there been a case of the sovereign loving benevolence, and the people not loving righteousness. Never has there been a case where the people have loved righteousness, and the affairs of the sovereign have not been carried to completion. And never has there been a case where the wealth in such a State, collected in the treasuries and arsenals, did not continue in the sovereign's possession.

孟献子[1]曰:“畜马乘[2]不察于鸡豚,伐冰之家[3]不畜牛羊,百乘之家[4]不畜聚敛之臣，与其有聚敛之臣，宁有盗臣。”此谓国不以利为利，以义为利也。长[5]国家而务财用者，必自[6]小人矣。彼为善之，小人之使为国家，菑害并至。虽有善者，亦无如之何[7]矣！此谓国不以利为利，以义为利也。

---

1. 孟献子：仲孙蔑，春秋时期鲁国外交家、政治家。
2. 畜马乘：指士大夫之家。
3. 伐冰之家：指卿大夫以上之家，源自其丧祭用冰。
4. 百乘之家：有采地者，指诸侯之家。
5. 长（zhǎng）：成为……之长。
6. 自：由，指受小人诱导。
7. 无如之何：没有任何办法。

22. The officer Meng Xian said, "He who keeps horses and a carriage[1] does not look after fowls and pigs. The family which keeps its stores of ice[2] does not rear cattle or sheep. So, the house which possesses a hundred chariots[3] should not keep a minister to look out for imposts that he may lay them on the people. Than to have such a minister, it were better for that house to have one who should rob it of its revenues." This is in accordance with the saying: — "In a State, pecuniary gain is not to be considered prosperity, but its prosperity will be found in righteousness."

23. When he who presides over a State or a family makes revenues his chief business, he must be under the influence of some small, mean, man. He may consider this man to be good; but when such a person is employed in the administration of a State or family, calamities from Heaven, and injuries from men, will befall it together, and, though a good man may take his place, he will not be able to remedy the evil. This illustrates again the saying," In a State, gain is not to be considered prosperity, but its prosperity will be found in righteousness."

---

1. He who keeps horses and a carriage：理雅各没有翻译出原文“蓄马乘”的借代意义。如为了保留原文意象，可译为“He who keeps horses and a carriage, that is, a scholar-official”。
2. The family which keeps its stores of ice：同样，该句也具有借代意义，可译为“The family which keeps its stores of ice in funerals, that is, the family of a high minister or noble”。
3. the house which possesses a hundred chariots：可改译为“the house which possesses a hundred chariots, that is, the house of a duke or a prince”。

《大学》术语汇编与简释

大学：the Great Learning

对于“大学”，郑玄和朱熹有不同的解释。郑玄认为，“大学者，以其记博学可以为政也。”大学就是广博的学习。朱熹则认为，“大学者乃大人之学也”，古人八岁入小学，学习日常的洒扫应对进退之节仪，十五岁入大学，以公卿大夫贵族子弟与庶民之俊秀者为主，学习进德修业治人的大道理。总体而言，大学属于成人性质的教育，以修养品德和将来治人从政为目的。（陈生玺，2013）

明德：illustrious virtue

朱熹认为，“明德者，人之所得乎天，而虚灵不昧，以具众理而应万事者也。但为气禀所拘，人欲所蔽，则有时而昏；然其本体之明，则有未尝息者。故学者当因其所发而遂明之，以复其初也。”所以，明德指人自身的光明德性，是人本性中存在的一种纯洁光明的德性，但由于后天受社会习染会产生各种不良的欲念，教育的目的就是要人们认识恢复自身的这种德性，革除一切不良的污染，成为新人，从思想品德和行为上达到完美至善的境地。

新（亲）民：to renovate the people

如“明德”所示，“新民”就是要革除因后天受社会习染而产生的各种不良欲念，从而恢复自身纯洁光明的德性，进而成为新人。简而言之，新民即弃旧图新，去恶从善。

至善：highest excellence, the

事理当然之极也。言明明德、新民，皆当至于至善之地而不迁。盖必其有以尽夫天理之极，而无一毫人欲之私也。也就是说，要求人们从思想品德和行为上达到完美至善的境地。为人君，止于仁；为人臣，止于敬；为人子，止于孝；为人父，止于慈；与国人交，止于信。仁、敬、孝、慈、信就是不同身份之人的至善之行。

格物：investigation of things

按照朱熹的解释，“穷至事物之理，欲其极处无不到也。”也就是说，探究事物的原理，直至彻底清楚明白。

致知：extension of knowledge

使认识达到极点，即认识明确，推极吾之知识，欲其所知无不尽也。

诚意：sincere in thoughts

意念真诚，实其心之所发，欲其一于善而无自欺也。

正心：to rectify their hearts

心者，身之所主也。正心就是要消除内心的忿懥、恐惧、好乐和忧患。

修身：to cultivate their persons

人会因为其所亲爱、其所贱恶、其所畏敬、其所哀矜、其所敖惰而有失偏颇，所以人要努力做到好而知其恶，恶而知其美，这就是修身。简而言之，修身就是要修养好自身的品德。

齐家：to regulate their families

安定自己的家庭，使家族齐心协力，平安和睦。家在这里指家族，古代卿大夫可统治一定的地域，组成以血缘关系为纽带的家族，不同于现代意义上的“家”或“家庭”。齐家，首先自身要修好品德，做到孝、悌、慈，以修身而教于家。

治国：to order well their States

治理诸侯国。治国与齐家具有同样的道理，就是要使民众做到孝、悌和不倍。君子的行为应起到示范作用，所以要“上老老，上长长，上恤孤”，民众自然就会跟从，兴起孝道和悌道，也不会背叛。

平天下：to illustrate illustrious virtue throughout the empire

天下指周王朝统御包括各诸侯国的整个中国。所以，平天下就是平定整个中国，要以修养自身的品德为根本，要让光明的德行兴盛于天下。

絜矩之道：The principle, with which, as with a measuring square, to regulate one’s conduct

儒家伦理思想之一，指君子的一言一行要有示范作用。絜，度量。矩，画方形或直角的用具。按文中的解释，絜矩之道就是要做到“所恶于上，毋以使下；所恶于下，毋以事上；所恶于前，毋以先后；所恶于后，毋以从前；所恶于右，毋以交于左；所恶于左，毋以交于右。”

《中庸》导读

杨文地

《中庸》同《大学》一样，出自《礼记》，原为《礼记》的第三十一篇，相传为战国时期孔子的孙子子思（公元前483年—前402年）所作。在《中庸》的注疏史上，最具代表性的人物是汉代经学家郑玄和宋代理学家朱熹，但二者所处时代、所属学派皆不同，其对儒学的理解存在差异，因此由他们建构或展示的《中庸》思想也各不相同。朱熹终其一生整理注疏“四书”，重新建构了儒家思想，对《中庸》的思想体系进行了明确说明，故本书注释以其《中庸章句》作为底本。根据朱熹的观点，《中庸》在“四书”中应最后阅读，作为“孔门心法”，它是儒家思想体系中最具哲学性、最形而上的部分，因此也是最难读懂的部分。

朱熹认为，“读书先须看大纲，又看几多间架。如‘天命之谓性，率性之谓道，修道之谓教’，此是大纲。夫妇所知所能，与圣人不知不能处，此类是间架。譬人看屋，先看他大纲，次看几多间，间内又有小间，然后方得贯通。”要想把握《中庸》的思想，就得掌握其论述逻辑，而这正是难点所在，对其进行结构分析无疑是攻克难点的最佳途径。朱熹将《中庸》划分为五大部分共三十三章，并对每章做了内容总结。但是，这种表面的结构划分无法体现书中庞杂内容的内在论述逻辑，加之作者的不确定性，

《中庸》作为篇章的完整性曾受到质疑，其结构和思想表达婉转曲折，对当代读者构成了很大的挑战。

《中庸》之所以难理解主要有两方面的原因。首先，其表达方式属于文章学式的论证结构，表面逻辑关系不明，思维发展是非线性的，用简洁的语言表达了多个层次，具有诗学精神，强调人的内在共鸣，突出整体感受，必须通过整体阅读方式来把握，经过综合性的交流才能理解。其次，文化和历史差距带来的阅读困难，对国人来说如此，对外国人而言更甚。科举时代的读者从小耳濡目染，反复默记，加之环境的儒家取向，文本的相互印证，理解上相对容易。而对于现代读者，特别是外国读者，《中庸》赖以存在的语境不足以提供足够的信息，其论证的思维逻辑与西方的线性逻辑相差甚远，单纯的字面解释无法清晰地阐释其论证思想。所以，对《中庸》的理解必须通过整体阅读，抓住其中的几个关键论点，再围绕这些论点将纷繁复杂的论证条分缕析，归于原位。

《中庸》的主要论点体现在开篇的三句话之中，其总体思想可概述如下：

开篇以"天命之谓性，率性之谓道，修道之谓教"为全书大纲确定了性、道、教三个定义，其源头是天，核心是教，主要是言人事。作为人事的修道典范是君子。其修道成功的表现是"中（原初内心）和（外在节制）"，产生的影响就是"天地位焉，万物育焉"。这是总的理想。

但现实情况是"民鲜能中庸久矣"，原因是"过"和"不及"并存，但舜是成功的典范；"道之不行"，原因是不明道，不能守，但颜回是成功的典范。那么，究竟怎么做才能实现中庸？以君子为例明示：和而不流、中立不倚、忠贞坚守、不求名利。道既费且隐，费是用，是现象；隐是体，是理，是规律。修道要正心，居易俟命，从近处身边做起，处理好五种人际关系（五达道，或五常、五伦，即父子、君臣、夫妇、兄弟、朋友关系），其原则是“己所不欲勿施于人”。这就需要修炼各种品德，尤其是知、仁、勇三德。“好学近乎知，力行近乎仁，知耻近乎勇”。这个过程包含三知（生而知之、学而知之、困而知之）和三行（安而行之、利而行之、勉强而行之），但都归结为“诚”。作为君王的君子，治理国家需遵循九经（修身、尊贤、亲亲、敬大臣、体群臣、子庶民、来百工、柔远人、怀诸侯），其核心依然是“诚”。

“诚”有诚者和诚之者之分，即天道和人道。“诚者不勉而中，不思而得，从容中道”，乃圣人所为，非常人之所及，因此人们可转而追求人道，“诚之者择善而固执之”。具体做法就是“博学之，审问之，慎思之，明辨之，笃行之”，就是要“人一能之，己百之；人十能之，己千之”，持之以恒，坚持不懈，直待得仁、义、礼、智与忠孝之道，日用实理，然后为诚。只有天下至诚之人，才能充分发挥他的本性，从而发挥大众的本性，以至发挥万物的本性，最终帮助天地化育生命，与天地并列共存。即诚者，除了自我完善，还需完善事物，以修得仁和知，做到内外兼修、以时措之，并最终达到至诚，“经纶天下之大经，立天下之大本，知天地之化育”，也就实现了开篇的理想境界。

“中庸”的内涵可以理解为“中和”，如《中庸》开篇的论述，就是要在处理事物时不偏不倚，使人和谐相处。但日常人伦复杂且难以穿透，内外部因素诸多，要做到“时中”这一理想境界难度极大，而以纯粹不受遮蔽的状态达成中庸则更难。虽然不易，但也绝非没有可能，这就要求人们通过修身，即道德修养，恢复原初善的本性，成为君子，处理好各种人际关系，做到“诚”。这实际上就是《中庸》论述的三个主题：君子、社群、诚，体现的是“仁”“义”“礼”的统一，反映了《中庸》中存在的完整人文主义理念，即天人合一，通过人的自身努力，成就自己、成就他人，实现人生的终极筹划。其中，“仁”“义”“礼”构成一套高度浓缩的复杂预设结构，“仁”的亲情和“义”的公正通过“礼”的规则来实现，“礼”是“仁”“义”在人际关系脉络中实现的动态结构，是人化的过程，是融入社会的过程，是培植发展种种人际关系的过程。“仁”“义”“礼”三者之间相互协调和推进，最终实现自我转化。《中庸》表明，儒家提倡人们必须作有意识的和诚心的努力，以保证可以察觉人类社群所有成员共有的普遍性（庸），并听到其内心所发出的旋律。

《中庸》的教育意义体现在博学、审问、慎思、明辨、笃行之中，反映了教育在书中的中心地位。《中庸》倡导的教育不是外界强加的，而是人们自愿参与的。教育本身建立在学习者道德决心基础之上，学习者的老师就是自己，“教”实际上是一种自我启迪或昭明的过程，对自我意识的追求可理解为对知天的相应追求。这就是《中庸》中所体现的理想教育，符合孟子“知性则可以知天”的思想。

相比《大学》而言，《中庸》的价值更胜一筹。朱熹说：“某要人先读大学，以定其规模；次读论语，以立其根本；次读孟子，以观其发越；次读中庸，以求古人之微妙（处）。”《大学》是儒学入门读物，而《中庸》则体现了儒学的微妙之处。子思作《中庸》的目的是“忧道学之失其传而作也。盖自上古圣神继天立极，而道统之传有自来矣。其见于经，则‘允执厥中’者，尧之所以授舜也；‘人心惟危，道心惟微，惟精惟一，允执厥中’者，舜之所以授禹也。尧之一言，至矣，尽矣！而舜复益之以三言者，则所以明夫尧之一言，必如是而后可庶几也。”《中庸》是道学的核心，是“孔门传授心法”，“其书始言一理，中散为万事，末复合为一理，‘放之则弥六合，卷之则退藏于密’，其味无穷，皆实学也。善读者玩索而有得焉，则终身用之，有不能尽者矣。”

“中庸”是儒家重要的道德准则，是其为人处世的最高规范，对古代儒家思想体系的完善和儒学教育的延续产生了深远影响。中庸思想在儒家思想中的核心地位并非一蹴而就，在孔子之前的典籍，如《尚书》（人心惟危，道心惟微，惟精惟一，允执厥中）、《周易》（得尚于中行、中以为实也）、《左传》（民受天地之中以生，所谓命也）、《周礼》（以刑教中），都存在与中庸有关的思想论述，而孔子在先贤基础之上总结并加以创新，集中论述了中庸思想，如《中庸》文中孔子语。另外，在其他中国古代经典中也常见类似“守中”和“执中”的概念，如《庄子》（中道、养中）、《韩非子》（去甚去泰，身乃无害）、《管子》（中正者，治之本也）等。这说明，中庸思想不仅是儒家思想的核心，也是中华民族精神世界的核心所在，它已成为一种集体无意识，化为中华民族血脉的一部分。

中庸

The Doctrine of the Mean[1]

1. The Doctrine of the Mean：理雅各自己承认，他将“中庸”译为“The Doctrine of the Mean”实际上只翻译了第一个字“中”。对于“中庸”的理解和注释一直存在分歧，朱熹认为，“中者，不偏不倚、无过不及之名。庸，平常也。”“中”和“庸”不是截然分开的，“庸”只是“中”的“常然而不易”，“中”要得“常”，二者“一经一纬”，缺一不可。“中庸”二字虽各有其意，实则彼此相通，互为补充，二者兼具才可实现其完整意义。但是，要想在英文中确切传达“中庸”的含义，做到二者兼顾，异常困难，后期一些译者做过多种尝试，如“Kung Yung or The State of Equilibrium and Harmony”（Legge, 1885）兼顾“中和”；“The Universal Order, or Conduct of Life”（Ku，1906）跳出原文从整体理解；“Focusing the Familiar”（Ames & Hall, 2001）强调“庸”；“Maintaining Perfect Balance”（Gardner, 2007）突出整体含义等等，但仍无法做到尽善尽美，或多或少总有所缺憾。

第一章

天命[1]之谓性，率[2]性之谓道，修[3]道之谓教[4]。道也者，不可须臾离[5]也，可离非道也。是故君子戒慎乎其所不睹，恐惧乎其所不闻。

1. 命：令，赋予。
2. 率：遵循。
3. 修：（根据品性）加以节制、划分。
4. 教：礼、乐、刑、政等教化措施。
5. 离：去声，表被动。

1. What Heaven has conferred is called THE NATURE; an accordance with this nature is called THE PATH of duty[1]; the regulation of this path[2] is called INSTRUCTION[3].

2. The path may not be left for an instant. If it could be left, it would not be the path. On this account, the superior man does not wait till he sees things, to be cautious, nor till he hears things, to be apprehensive.

---

1. THE PATH of duty：这个翻译具有宗教意义。在中国哲学中，作为抽象的“道”引申为“人或物所必须遵循的轨道，通称为道。日月星辰所遵循的轨道称为天道，人类生活所遵循的轨道称为人道”。宋代思想家们认为“道就是物质世界的总过程”，清王夫之采纳了程朱观点，认为道就是“天地人物的普遍规律”。“道”包含过程与规律的意义，都是客观世界的反映。在《中庸》中，“道”是普遍的规律，是体用结合体，既费且隐，有天道和人道之分。所以，“道”更为常见的翻译是“Way”，或者直接用汉语拼音“Dao”。
2. the regulation of this path：“修道”是指“遵循道的规律修养自己”。译文“the regulation of this path”变成对道的调节、修正，逻辑关系错误。不妨译为“cultivating onself along the Way”。
3. INSTRUCTION：将“教”译为“instruction”缩小了意义，突出了被动接受教育，“教”可分主动和被动两个方面，而儒家思想的“修身”主动含义更强，不妨译作“education”。

莫见[1]乎隐，莫显乎微，故君子慎其独也。喜怒哀乐之未发，谓之中[2]；发而皆中节[3]，谓之和[4]。中也者，天下之大本[5]也；和也者，天下之达道[6]也。致[7]中和，天地位[8]焉，万物育[9]焉。

1. 见（xiàn）：同“现”，显现。
2. 中：不偏不倚。
3. 中节：合乎礼义法度。
4. 和：不乖戾。
5. 大本：根本，天命之性。
6. 达道：规律。
7. 致：达到。
8. 位：安于其位。
9. 育：顺心生长。

3. There is nothing more visible than what is secret, and nothing more manifest than what is minute. Therefore the superior man[1] is watchful over himself, when he is alone[2].

4. While there are no stirrings of pleasure, anger, sorrow, or joy, the mind may be said to be in the state of EQUILIBRIUM. When those feelings have been stirred, and they act in their due degree, there ensues what may be called the state of HARMONY. This EQUILIBRIUM is the great root from which grow all the human actings in the world, and this HARMONY is the universal path[3] which they all should pursue.

5. Let the states of equilibrium and harmony exist in perfection, and a happy order will prevail throughout heaven and earth, and all things will be nourished and flourish.

---

1. the superior man："君子"在中国古代有两层含义，一是从地位来看，在上位的人称为"君子"，一般平民被称为"小人"；另一层含义是从品德上来判断，指品德高尚之人。"superior man"突出地位。在《大学》和《中庸》中，语境的不同，"君子"的含义也有所不同，不能一概译为"superior man"。指"品德高尚"时可译为"moral man""morally noble man""exemplary person"，或者直接用汉语拼音"junzi"。
2. when he is alone：与《大学》里"慎独"的注释相比，《中庸》里"慎独"的语境信息更为丰富，"君子戒慎乎其所不睹，恐惧乎其所不闻。莫见乎隐，莫显乎微"，只有一个人的内心深处才是自己看不见、听不见，但又明显能感受到的地方，是他人不知而自己独知之处，所以常需戒备，恐其变化。"独"译为"when he is alone"显然无法体现这层含义，不妨译作"his secret thoughts""his secret self"，或者"his inner self"。
3. the universal path：理雅各采用直译，喻指普遍规律，可改译为"the universal law or principle"。

第二章

仲尼曰："君子中庸，小人反中庸。君子之中庸也，君子而时[1]中；小人之中庸也[2]，小人而无忌惮也。"

---

1. 时：随时。
2. 小人之中庸也：朱熹赞同王肃的观点，认为此处应为"小人之反中庸也。"

1. Zhongni[1] said, "The superior man embodies the course of the Mean; the mean man acts contrary to the course of the Mean.

2. "The superior man's embodying the course of the Mean is because he is a superior man, and so always maintains the Mean. The mean man's acting contrary to the course of the Mean is because he is a mean man, and has no caution."

1. Zhongni：指孔子，不妨统一译作"Confucius"。

第三章

子曰："中庸其至[1]矣乎！民鲜能[2]久矣！"

---

1. 至：极致。
2. 能：《论语》中该句没有"能"字。

The Master[1] said, "Perfect is the virtue which is according to the Mean! Rare have they long been among the people, who could practice it!"

1. The Master：指孔子，可统一译作"Confucius"，下同。

第四章

子曰："道之不行也，我知之矣，知[1]者过之，愚者不及也；道之不明也，我知之矣，贤者过之，不肖者不及也。人莫不饮食也，鲜能知味也。"

1. 知：去声，同"智"。

1. The Master said, "I know how it is that the path of the Mean is not walked in: — The knowing go beyond it, and the stupid do not come up to it. I know how it is that the path of the Mean is not understood: — The men of talents and virtue go beyond it, and the worthless do not come up to it.

2. "There is no body but eats and drinks. But they are few who can distinguish flavors."

第五章

子曰："道其不行矣夫！"[1]

1. 子曰："道其不行矣夫！"：孔子说："唉，中庸之道大概不能实行了吧！"

The Master said, “Alas! How is the path of the Mean untrodden!” [1]

1. Alas! How is the path of the Mean untrodden!：为了更清楚地表达原文含义，可译为 “What a pity! The doctrine of the mean will probably never be practised”。

第六章

子曰："舜其大知[1]也与！舜好问而好察迩言[2]，隐恶而扬善，执其两端，用其中于民，其斯以为舜乎！"

1. 知：去声，同"智"。
2. 迩言：浅显的话。

The Master said, “There was Shun: — He indeed was greatly wise! Shun loved to question others, and to study their words, though they might be shallow. He concealed[1] what was bad in them and displayed what was good. He took hold of their two extremes, determined the Mean[2], and employed it in his government of the people. It was by this that he was Shun!”

---

1. concealed：“隐”从字面含义考虑确实可以译为“conceal”，但是从语境判断，舜对人们的关注点在好的地方而不是做得不好之处，对于“恶”，他不去宣扬而已，而非可以隐瞒，所以将“隐”译为“disregard”“keep...concealed”，或者“pass over”更能体现舜的良苦用心。
2. the Mean：“用中于民”并非取两端中点或者折中，而是在两个极端之间找到最佳平衡点，即解决问题的最佳办法，所以“中”不妨译为“the best way”，或者“the perfect balance”。

第七章

子曰："人皆曰予知，驱而纳诸罟[1]擭[2]陷阱之中，而莫之知辟[3]也。人皆曰予知，择乎中庸而不能期月[4]守也。"

1. 罟（gǔ）：网。
2. 擭（huò）：机槛。
3. 辟：同"避"。
4. 期（jī）月：一个月。

The Master said, "Men all say, 'We are wise'; but being driven forward and taken in a net, a trap, or a pitfall, they know not how to escape. Men all say, 'We are wise'; but happening to choose the course of the Mean, they are not able to keep it for a round month."

第八章

子曰："回[1]之为人也，择乎中庸，得一善，则拳拳[2]服膺[3]而弗失之矣。"

---

1. 回：颜回。
2. 拳拳：奉持珍惜的样子。
3. 服膺：著于心胸之间，指牢记于心。服：著，拿着。膺：胸。

The Master said, "This was the manner of Hui: — he made choice of the Mean, and whenever he got hold of what was good, he clasped it firmly, as if wearing it on his breast, and did not lose it."

第九章

子曰：“天下国家可均[1]也，爵禄可辞也，白刃可蹈也，中庸不可能也。”

---

1. 均：治理，整顿。

The Master said, "The empire, its States, and its families, may be perfectly ruled; dignities[1] and emoluments[2] may be declined; naked weapons may be trampled under the feet; — but the course of the Mean cannot be attained to."

---

1. dignities："爵"指爵位、官位，"dignity"特指"高位、显职"，也可译为"official titles"。
2. emoluments：俸给。

第十章

子路问强。子曰："南方之强与？北方之强与？抑[1]而[2]强与？宽柔以教，不报[3]无道[4]，南方之强也，君子居之。衽[5]金革[6]，死而不厌，北方之强也，而强者居之。故君子和而不流[7]，强哉矫！中立而不倚，强哉矫！国有道，不变塞[8]焉，强哉矫！国无道，至死不变，强哉矫！"

---

1. 抑：还是。
2. 而：你。
3. 报：报复。
4. 无道：不行正道（的坏人）。
5. 衽（rèn）：以……为席。
6. 金革：兵器和甲胄。
7. 流：随波逐流，盲从他人。
8. 塞：未达，指未达之志。

1. Zilu asked about energy[1].

2. The Master said, "Do you mean the energy of the South, the energy of the North, or the energy which you should cultivate yourself?

3. "To show forbearance and gentleness in teaching others; and not to revenge unreasonable conduct: — this is the energy of Southern regions, and the good man makes it his study.

4. "To lie under arms; and meet death without regret: — this is the energy of Northern regions, and the forceful make it their study.

5. "Therefore, the superior man cultivates a friendly harmony, without being weak[2]. — How firm is he in his energy! He stands erect in the middle, without inclining to either side. — How firm is he in his energy! When good principles prevail in the government of his country, he does not change from what he was in retirement. — How firm is he in his energy! When bad principles prevail in the country, he maintains his course to death without changing. — How firm is he in his energy!"

---

1. energy：子路好勇，所以问"强"。"强"指"强大、刚毅"。"energy"指"精力"，对"强"的表现力不足，不妨译作"strength"，或者"power"。
2. without being weak：原文"流"是指"随波逐流，盲从他人"，不妨译作"without following others blindly"。

第十一章

子曰:“素[1]隐[2]行怪[3]，后世有述焉，吾弗为之矣。君子遵道而行，半涂而废，吾弗能已[4]矣。君子依乎中庸，遁世不见知而不悔，唯圣者能之。

1. 素：应为“索”，探求。
2. 隐：精深，玄妙。
3. 怪：诡异，怪异。
4. 已：停止。

1. The Master said, "To live in obscurity[1], and yet practice wonders[2], in order to be mentioned with honor in future ages: — this is what I do not do.

2. "The good man[3] tries to proceed according to the right path, but when he has gone halfway, he abandons it: — I am not able so to stop.

3. "The superior man accords with the course of the Mean. Though he may be all unknown, unregarded by the world, he feels no regret. — It is only the sage who is able for this."

---

1. To live in obscurity："隐"在此处作"精深、玄妙"解；"素"应为"索"，"追求"之意。所以该句改译为"to seek for abstruse"。
2. wonders："行怪"指"做一些怪异之事"，所以"怪"不妨译作"the eccentric"。
3. The good man：因其半途而废，与真正的君子（the superior man）区分开来，指有心向善、试图提升自身品德之人。

第十二章

君子之道费[1]而隐[2]。夫妇[3]之愚，可以与知焉，及其至也，虽圣人亦有所不知焉；夫妇之不肖，可以能行焉，及其至也，虽圣人亦有所不能焉。天地之大也，人犹有所憾[4]。故君子语大，天下莫能载焉；语小，天下莫能破焉。诗云："鸢[5]飞戾[6]天，鱼跃于渊。"言其上下察[7]也。君子之道，造端乎夫妇；及其至也，察乎天地。

1. 费：广大，指用之广。
2. 隐：精微，指体之微。
3. 夫妇：男男女女，指普通人。
4. 憾：不满。
5. 鸢（yuān）：鹞鹰。
6. 戾：至，到。
7. 察：显著。

1. The way which the superior man pursues reaches wide and far, and yet is secret[1].

2. Common men and women, however ignorant, may intermeddle with the knowledge of it; yet in its utmost reaches, there is that which even the sage does not know. Common men and women, however much below the ordinary standard of character, can carry it into practice; yet in its utmost reaches, there is that which even the sage is not able to carry into practice. Great as heaven and earth are, men still find some things in them with which to be dissatisfied. Thus it is that, were the superior man to speak of his way in all its greatness, nothing in the world would be found able to embrace it, and were he to speak of it in its minuteness, nothing in the world would be found able to split it.

3. It is said in the Book of Poetry, "The hawk flies up to heaven; the fishes leap in the deep." This expresses how this way is seen above and below.

4. The way of the superior man may be found, in its simple elements, in the intercourse of common men and women; but in its utmost reaches, it shines brightly through heaven and earth.

---

1. secret：结合上下文，可改译为"minute and subtle"。

第十三章

子曰："道不远人。人之为道而远人，不可以为道。诗[1]云：'伐柯[2]伐柯，其则[3]不远。'执柯以伐柯，睨[4]而视之，犹以为远[5]。故君子以人治人，改而止。

1. 诗：《诗经·豳风·伐柯》。
2. 伐柯：伐木做斧柄。柯：斧柄。
3. 则：法则，样式。
4. 睨：斜着眼看。
5. 远：这里指有差别，不一样。

1. The Master said, "The path is not far from man. When men try to pursue a course, which is far from the common indications of consciousness, this course cannot be considered THE PATH.[1]

2. "In the Book of Poetry, it is said, 'In hewing an axe-handle, in hewing an axe-handle, the pattern is not far off.' We grasp one axe handle to hew the other; and yet, if we look askance from the one to the other, we may consider them as apart.[2] Therefore, the superior man governs men, according to their nature, with what is proper to them, and as soon as they change what is wrong, he stops.

---

1. When men try to pursue a course ... this course cannot be considered THE PATH："人之为道而远人，不可以为道"指修道之人如果认为日常身边之事不足以修道而追求高远难行之事的话就不可以修道，因为如《中庸》开篇所说"率性之谓道"，道乃率性而已，是众人能知能行之事，不会远于人。该句翻译的问题是变换了行为主体，指修道之人而非道。此句可译为"The man that makes a way and does away with man, cannot make the Way"(Lyall & King, 1927)，或者"If a man pursues a way which removes him from men, he cannot be in The Way"(Hughes, 1943/1979)。
2. We grasp one axe handle ... we may consider them as apart：该句可改译为"We take hold of one axe handle to hew another. Yet when we look at them carefully, we find that they are still different"。

忠恕[1]违道不远，施诸己而不愿，亦勿施于人。君子之道四，丘未能一焉：所求[2]乎子，以事[3]父未能也；所求乎臣，以事君未能也；所求乎弟，以事兄未能也；所求乎朋友，先施之未能也。庸[4]德之行，庸言之谨，有所不足，不敢不勉，有余不敢尽；言顾行，行顾言，君子胡不慥慥[5]尔！”

1. 忠恕：儒家的道德规范。忠：尽己之心。恕：推己及人。
2. 求：要求。
3. 事：对待，侍奉。
4. 庸：平常。
5. 慥慥：敦厚老实。

3. "When one cultivates to the utmost the principles of his nature, and exercises them on the principle of reciprocity, he is not far from the path. What you do not like when done to yourself, do not do to others.[1]

4. "In the way of the superior man there are four things, to not one of which have I as yet attained. — To serve my father, as I would require my son to serve me: to this I have not attained; to serve my prince, as I would require my minister to serve me: to this I have not attained; to serve my elder brother, as I would require my younger brother to serve me: to this I have not attained; to set the example in behaving to a friend, as I would require him to behave to me: to this I have not attained. Earnest in practicing the ordinary virtues, and careful in speaking about them, if, in his practice, he has anything defective, the superior man dares not but exert himself; and if, in his words, he has any excess, he dares not allow himself such license. Thus his words have respect to his actions, and his actions have respect to his words; is it not just an entire sincerity which marks the superior man?"

---

1. What you do not like when done to yourself, do not do to others："己所不欲勿施于人"的其他几种译文：What you do not wish others should do unto you, do not do unto them (Ku, 1906); What you do not wish others to do to you, do not do to them (Chan, 1963); What you do not like done to yourself, do not do to others (Chai & Chai, 1965); Do not treat others as you yourself would not wish to be treated (Ames & Hall, 2001)。

第十四章

君子素[1]其位而行，不愿[2]乎其外。素富贵，行乎富贵；素贫贱，行乎贫贱；素夷狄，行乎夷狄；素患难，行乎患难；君子无入而不自得焉。在上位不陵[3]下，在下位不援[4]上，正己而不求于人则无怨。上不怨天，下不尤人。故君子居易[5]以俟命，小人行险以徼[6]幸[7]。子曰："射有似乎君子；失诸正鹄[8]，反求诸其身。"

---

1. 素：犹见在，引申为根据。
2. 愿：羡慕。
3. 陵：同"凌"，欺负。
4. 援：同"缘"，攀缘，巴结。
5. 居易：即前文的"素位而行"。
6. 徼：求。
7. 幸：不应获得的东西。
8. 鹄（gǔ）：箭靶的中心，泛指靶子。

1. The superior man does what is proper to the station in which he is; he does not desire to go beyond this.

2. In a position of wealth and honor, he does what is proper to a position of wealth and honor. In a poor and low position, he does what is proper to a poor and low position. Situated among barbarous tribes, he does what is proper to a situation among barbarous tribes. In a position of sorrow and difficulty, he does what is proper to a position of sorrow and difficulty. The superior man can find himself in no situation in which he is not himself.

3. In a high situation, he does not treat with contempt his inferiors. In a low situation, he does not court the favor of his superiors. He rectifies himself, and seeks for nothing from others, so that he has no dissatisfactions. He does not murmur against Heaven, nor grumble against men.

4. Thus it is that the superior man is quiet and calm, waiting for the appointments of Heaven, while the mean man walks in dangerous paths, looking for lucky occurrences.

5. The Master said, "In archery we have something like the way of the superior man. When the archer misses the center of the target, he turns round and seeks for the cause of his failure in himself."

第十五章

君子之道，辟[1]如行远必自迩[2]，辟如登高必自卑[3]。诗[4]曰："妻子好合，如鼓瑟琴；兄弟既翕[5]，和乐且耽[6]；宜尔室家，乐尔妻帑[7]。"子曰："父母其顺矣乎！"

1. 辟：同"譬"，譬如。
2. 迩：近。
3. 卑：低。
4. 诗：《诗经·小雅·常棣》。
5. 翕：合。
6. 耽：《诗经》中为"湛"，意"乐"。
7. 帑（nú）：同"孥"，指儿女。

1. The way of the superior man may be compared to what takes place in traveling, when to go far we must traverse the space that is near, and in ascending a height we must begin from the lower ground.

2. It is said in the Book of Poetry, "Happy union with wife and children is like the music of lutes and harps.[1] When there is concord among brethren, the harmony is delightful and enduring. Thus may you regulate your family, and enjoy the pleasure of your wife and children.[2]"

3. The Master said, "In such a state of things, parents have entire complacence!"

---

1. Happy union with wife and children is like the music of lutes and harps：对于《诗经·小雅·常棣》片段的引用旨在说明"行远自迩、登高自卑"，原诗勾画的是一幅兄弟和乐、骨肉相亲、夫妻和睦、全家团圆的景象。"妻子好合，如鼓瑟琴"应该是指妻子和孩子之间的融洽关系，"兄弟既翕，和乐且耽"也是表达这种融洽关系，而这正是君子齐家的结果，即"宜尔室家，乐尔妻帑"。所以，前面描写的场景是指家庭成员之间而非单指君子与家庭成员之间的关系，该句不妨译为"Wife and children are loving and concordant like the strumming of the zither and lute" (Riegel, 1978)。
2. Thus may you regulate your family, and enjoy the pleasure of your wife and children：结合以上注释，该句改译为"Thus may you regulate your family and make them live in concord and bring your wife and children delight"。

第十六章

子曰："鬼神之为德，其盛矣乎！视之而弗见，听之而弗闻，体物而不可遗。使天下之人齐[1]明盛服,以承祭祀。洋洋乎[2]！如在其上,如在其左右。诗[3]曰:'神之格思[4],不可度思！矧[5]可射[6]思!'夫微之显，诚之不可掩如此夫。"

1. 齐（zhāi）：通"斋"，庄重，严肃恭敬，指古人在祭祀或其他典礼前整洁身心，以示庄敬。
2. 洋洋乎：此处指鬼神像萦绕在周围一样。
3. 诗：《诗经・大雅・抑》。
4. 格思：降临。
5. 矧（shěn）：况且。
6. 射（yì）：厌弃。

1. The Master said, "How abundantly do spiritual beings display the powers that belong to them!

2. "We look for them, but do not see them; we listen to them, but do not hear them; yet they enter into all things, and there is nothing without them.

3. "They cause all the people in the empire to fast and purify themselves, and array themselves in their richest dresses, in order to attend at their sacrifices. Then, like overflowing water, they seem to be over the heads, and on the right and left of their worshippers.

4. "It is said in the Book of Poetry, 'The approaches of the spirits, you cannot surmise; and can you treat them with indifference?'

5. "Such is the manifestness of what is minute! Such is the impossibility of repressing the outgoings of sincerity[1]!"

---

1. sincerity：汉语"诚"和英语"sincerity"在字面意义上比较相近，都指对自我的真实，是赢得他人信任的基础，但是从哲学意义上来说，"诚"的概念要远大于"sincerity"，直指人的真实所在，是人自我认识和参与天地化育的基础，是天人合一的源动力。而"sincerity"在英语中是个中性词，甚至有负面含义，只是强调"心口一致"。"诚"可以对应英语的多个概念，如"honesty""integrity""being true to oneself""creativity"等等，所以这样一个具有重要哲学意义的概念，不妨在翻译中不译，即选择使用汉语拼音"cheng"。

第十七章

子曰："舜其大孝也与！德为圣人，尊为天子，富有四海之内。宗庙飨[1]之，子孙保之。故大德必得其位，必得其禄，必得其名，必得其寿。故天之生物，必因其材而笃[2]焉。故栽者培之，倾者覆之。诗[3]曰：'嘉乐君子，宪宪[4]令德！宜民宜人，受禄于天；保佑命之，自天申[5]之！'故大德者必受命。"

---

1. 飨（xiǎng）：祭祀。
2. 笃：厚。
3. 诗：《诗经·大雅·假乐》。
4. 宪宪：应作"显显"，显明的样子。
5. 申：申斥，告诫。

1. The Master said, "How greatly filial was Shun! His virtue was that of a sage; his dignity was the throne; his riches were all within the four seas[1]. He offered his sacrifices in his ancestral temple, and his descendants preserved the sacrifices to himself.

2. "Therefore having such great virtue, it could not but be that he should obtain the throne, that he should obtain those riches, that he should obtain his fame, that he should attain to his long life.

3. "Thus it is that Heaven, in the production of things, is sure to be bountiful to them, according to their qualities. Hence the tree that is flourishing, it nourishes, while that which is ready to fall, it overthrows.

4. "In the Book of Poetry, it is said, 'The admirable amiable prince displayed conspicuously his excelling virtue, adjusting his people, and adjusting his officers. Therefore, he received from Heaven his emoluments of dignity. It protected him, assisted him, decreed him the throne; sending from Heaven these favors, as it were, repeatedly.'

5. "We may say therefore that he who is greatly virtuous will be sure to receive the appointment of Heaven."

---

1. the four seas：四海是我国古时所指东海、西海、南海和北海，泛指海内之地、全国各地。

第十八章

子曰："无忧者其惟文王乎！以王季为父，以武王为子，父作[1]之，子述[2]之。武王缵[3]大[4]王、王季、文王之绪[5]。壹戎衣[6]而有天下，身不失天下之显名。尊为天子，富有四海之内。宗庙飨之，子孙保之。武王末[7]受命，周公成文、武之德，追王大王、王季，上祀先公以天子之礼。斯礼也，达乎诸侯大夫，及士庶人。父为大夫，子为士，葬以大夫，祭以士。父为士，子为大夫，葬以士，祭以大夫。期[8]之丧达乎大夫，三年之丧达乎天子，父母之丧无贵贱一也。"

---

1. 作：积功累业。
2. 述：继承。
3. 缵（zuǎn）：继续。
4. 大：同"太"。
5. 绪：功业。
6. 戎衣：甲胄。此处指穿上战袍讨伐商纣王。
7. 末：晚年。
8. 期（jī）：一年。

1. The Master said, "It is only King Wen of whom it can be said that he had no cause for grief! His father was King Ji, and his son was King Wu. His father laid the foundations of his dignity, and his son transmitted it.

2. "King Wu continued the enterprise of King Tai, King Ji, and King Wen. He once buckled on his armor, and got possession of the empire. He did not lose the distinguished personal reputation which he had throughout the empire. His dignity was the royal throne. His riches were the possession of all within the four seas. He offered his sacrifices in his ancestral temple, and his descendants maintained the sacrifices to himself.

3. "It was in his old age that King Wu received the appointment to the throne, and the duke of Zhou completed the virtuous course of Wen and Wu. He carried up the title of king to Tai and Ji, and sacrificed to all the former dukes above them with the royal ceremonies. And this rule he extended to the princes of the empire, the great officers, the scholars, and the common people. If the father were a great officer and the son a scholar, then the burial was that due to a great officer, and the sacrifice that due to a scholar. If the father were a scholar and the son a great officer, then the burial was that due to a scholar, and the sacrifice that due to a great officer. The one year's mourning was made to extend only to the great officers, but the three years' mourning extended to the Son of Heaven[1]. In the mourning for a father or mother, he allowed no difference between the noble and the mean."

---

1. the Son of Heaven：天子，或译为"the Emperor"。

第十九章

子曰："武王、周公，其达孝矣乎！夫孝者：善继人之志，善述人之事者也。春秋，修其祖庙，陈其宗器，设其裳衣，荐其时食。宗庙之礼，所以序昭穆[1]也；序爵[2]，所以辨贵贱也；序事[3]，所以辨贤也；旅[4]酬[5]下为上，所以逮贱也；燕毛[6]，所以序齿也。

---

1. 昭穆：宗庙中的排列次序，左为昭，右为穆。
2. 爵：爵位。
3. 事：宗祝有司的职事。
4. 旅：众。
5. 酬：劝酒。
6. 燕毛：以头发的颜色区别长幼，安排坐次。燕：同"宴"。

1. The Master said, "How far-extending was the filial piety of King Wu and the duke of Zhou!

2. "Now filial piety is seen in the skillful carrying out of the wishes of our forefathers, and the skillful carrying forward of their undertakings.

3. "In spring and autumn, they repaired and beautified the temple-halls of their fathers[1], set forth their ancestral vessels, displayed their various robes, and presented the offerings of the several seasons.

4. "By means of the ceremonies of the ancestral temple, they distinguished the royal kindred according to their order of descent. By ordering the parties present according to their rank, they distinguished the more noble and the less. By the arrangement of the services, they made a distinction of talents and worth. In the ceremony of general pledging, the inferiors presented the cup to their superiors, and thus something was given the lowest to do. At the concluding feast, places were given according to the hair[2], and thus was made the distinction of years.

---

1. repaired and beautified the temple-halls of their fathers：可简化为"repaired the temple of their fathers"。
2. the hair："燕毛"指以毛发之色别长幼、为坐次，所以为进一步明确原文之意可改译为"the color of the hair"。

践其位，行其礼，奏其乐，敬其所尊，爱其所亲，事死如事生，事亡如事存，孝之至也。郊[1]社[2]之礼，所以事上帝也；宗庙之礼，所以祀乎其先也。明乎郊社之礼、禘[3]尝[4]之义，治国其如示[5]诸掌乎。”

1. 郊：祀天。
2. 社：祭地。
3. 禘（dì）：天子宗庙的大祭。
4. 尝：秋祭。
5. 示（shì）：通“视”，视诸掌，指易见，容易。

5. "They occupied the places of their forefathers, practiced their ceremonies, and performed their music. They reverenced those whom they honored, and loved those whom they regarded with affection. Thus they served the dead as they would have served them alive; they served the departed as they would have served them had they been continued among them.

6. "By the ceremonies of the sacrifices to Heaven and Earth they served God, and by the ceremonies of the ancestral temple they sacrificed to their ancestors. He who understands the ceremonies of the sacrifices to Heaven and Earth, and the meaning of the several sacrifices to ancestors, would find the government of a kingdom as easy as to look into his palm!"

第二十章

哀公[1]问政。子曰："文、武之政，布在方[2]策[3]。其人存，则其政举；其人亡，则其政息。人道敏[4]政，地道敏树。夫政也者，蒲卢[5]也。故为政在人，取人以身，修身以道，修道以仁。仁者人也，亲亲[6]为大；义者宜也，尊贤为大；亲亲之杀[7]，尊贤之等，礼所生也。在下位不获乎上，民不可得而治矣！[8]

---

1. 哀公：鲁国国君姬蒋。
2. 方：古代书写文字用的木板。
3. 策：古代用以记事的竹、木片，编在一起的叫"策"。亦借指书简，薄册。
4. 敏：迅速。
5. 蒲卢：蒲苇。
6. 亲亲：亲近、爱护亲人。
7. 杀（shài）：减少，降等。指亲族要按关系远近有所区别。
8. 在下位不获乎上，民不可得而治矣：根据郑玄的注释，该句出现在此处属误重，正确位置应在下文。

1. The Duke Ai asked about government.

2. The Master said, "The government of Wen and Wu is displayed in the records, — the tablets of wood and bamboo. Let there be the men and the government will flourish; but without the men, their government decays and ceases.[1]

3. "With the right men the growth of government is rapid, just as vegetation is rapid in the earth; and, moreover, their government might be called an easily-growing rush.

4. "Therefore the administration of government lies in getting proper men. Such men are to be got by means of the ruler's own character. That character is to be cultivated by his treading in the ways of duty. And the treading those ways of duty is to be cultivated by the cherishing of benevolence.

5. "Benevolence is the characteristic element of humanity, and the great exercise of it is in loving relatives. Righteousness is the accordance of actions with what is right, and the great exercise of it is in honoring the worthy. The decreasing measures of the love due to relatives, and the steps in the honor due to the worthy, are produced by the principle of propriety.

6. "When those in inferior situations do not possess the confidence of their superiors, they cannot retain the government of the people.

---

1. Let there be the men ... their government decays and ceases：此句翻译套用了《圣经》的经典句型。"其人存"中"人"指文王、武王，"其政举"中"政"指文王、武王的治国之政，所以为了上下文的衔接，该句可改译为"When they were alive, their system of government worked. When they were gone, their system of government also ceased to work"。

故君子不可以不修身；思修身，不可以不事亲；思事亲，不可以不知人；思知人，不可以不知天。”天下之达道[1]五，所以行之者三：曰君臣也，父子也，夫妇也，昆弟也，朋友之交也：五者天下之达道也。知、仁、勇三者，天下之达德[2]也，所以行之者一也。或生而知之，或学而知之，或困而知之，及其知之一也；或安而行之，或利而行之，或勉强而行之，及其成功一也。

---

1. 达道：天下共通的道理。
2. 达德：天下共通的品德。

7. “Hence the sovereign may not neglect the cultivation of his own character. Wishing to cultivate his character, he may not neglect to serve his parents. In order to serve his parents, he may not neglect to acquire a knowledge of men. In order to know men, he may not dispense with a knowledge of Heaven.

8. “The duties of universal obligation are five and the virtues wherewith they are practiced are three. The duties are those between sovereign and minister, between father and son, between husband and wife, between elder brother and younger, and those belonging to the intercourse of friends. Those five are the duties of universal obligation. Knowledge[1], magnanimity[2], and energy[3], these three, are the virtues universally binding. And the means by which they carry the duties into practice is singleness.

9. “Some are born with the knowledge of those duties; some know them by study; and some acquire the knowledge after a painful feeling of their ignorance. But the knowledge being possessed, it comes to the same thing. Some practice them with a natural ease; some from a desire for their advantages; and some by strenuous effort. But the achievement being made, it comes to the same thing.”

---

1. Knowledge：此处“知”通“智”，下文也解释“好学近乎知”，好学非智，但可破愚，所以改译为“wisdom”。
2. magnanimity：仁，为了与《大学》中“仁”的概念保持一致，此处可改译为“human kindness”。
3. energy：在“问强”部分，“强”的翻译理雅各也用了“energy”。如前所述，“强”体现的是“刚毅、坚强”，“勇”字表达“果敢、决断”，可译为“courage”或者“fortitude”。

子曰："好学近乎知，力行近乎仁，知耻近乎勇。知斯三者，则知所以修身；知所以修身，则知所以治人；知所以治人，则知所以治天下国家矣。"凡为天下国家有九经，曰：修身也，尊贤也，亲亲也，敬大臣也，体群臣也，子庶民也，来[1]百工也，柔[2]远人也，怀[3]诸侯也。

---

1. 来：后多做"徕"，招致，招揽。
2. 柔：怀柔，善待。
3. 怀：安，安抚。

10. The Master said, "To be fond of learning is to be near to knowledge. To practice with vigor is to be near to magnanimity. To possess the feeling of shame is to be near to energy.

11. "He who knows these three things knows how to cultivate his own character. Knowing how to cultivate his own character, he knows how to govern other men. Knowing how to govern other men, he knows how to govern the empire with all its States and families.

12. "All who have the government of the Empire with its States and families have nine standard rules to follow; — viz.[1], the cultivation of their own characters; the honoring of men of virtue and talents; affection towards their relatives; respect towards the great ministers; kind and considerate treatment of the whole body of officers; dealing with the mass of the people as children; encouraging the resort of all classes of artisans; indulgent treatment of men from a distance; and the kindly cherishing of the princes of the States.

1. viz.：即。

修身则道立，尊贤则不惑，亲亲则诸父昆弟不怨，敬大臣则不眩，体群臣则士之报礼重，子庶民则百姓劝[1]，来百工则财用足，柔远人则四方归之，怀诸侯则天下畏之。

1. 劝：勉励，规劝。

13. "By the ruler's cultivation of his own character, the duties of universal obligation are set forth. By honoring men of virtue and talents, he is preserved from errors of judgment. By showing affection to his relatives, there is no grumbling nor resentment among his uncles and brethren. By respecting the great ministers, he is kept from errors in the practice of government. By kind and considerate treatment of the whole body of officers, they are led to make the most grateful return for his courtesies. By dealing with the mass of the people as his children, they are led to exhort one another to what is good. By encouraging the resort of all classes of artisans, his resources for expenditure are rendered ample. By indulgent treatment of men from a distance, they are brought to resort to him from all quarters. And by kindly cherishing the princes of the States, the whole empire is brought to revere him.

齐明盛服，非礼不动，所以修身也；去谗远色，贱货而贵德，所以劝贤也；尊其位，重其禄，同其好恶，所以劝亲亲也；官盛任使，所以劝大臣也；忠信重禄，所以劝士也；时使薄敛，所以劝百姓也；日省月试，既禀[1]称事，所以劝百工也；送往迎来，嘉善而矜[2]不能，所以柔远人也；继绝世，举废国，治乱持危，朝[3]聘[4]以时，厚往而薄来[5]，所以怀诸侯也。

1. 既禀：古代官府发放的作为月薪的粮食，亦泛指薪俸。既：同“饩”(xì)。禀：同“廪”(lǐn)。
2. 矜：怜悯，同情。
3. 朝（cháo）：指诸侯见于天子。
4. 聘：指诸侯使大夫来献。
5. 厚往而薄来：指设宴赏赐的多，进献纳贡的少。

14. “Self-adjustment and purification, with careful regulation of his dress, and the not making a movement contrary to the rules of propriety: — this is the way for a ruler to cultivate his person. Discarding slanderers, and keeping himself from the seductions of beauty; making light of riches, and giving honor to virtue: — this is the way for him to encourage men of worth and talents. Giving them places of honor and large emolument, and sharing with them in their likes and dislikes: — this is the way for him to encourage his relatives to love him[1]. Giving them numerous officers to discharge their orders and commissions: — this is the way for him to encourage the great ministers. According to them a generous confidence, and making their emoluments large: — this is the way to encourage the body of officers. Employing them only at the proper times, and making the imposts light: — this is the way to encourage the people. By daily examinations and monthly trials, and by making their rations in accordance with their labors: — this is the way to encourage the classes of artisans. To escort them on their departure and meet them on their coming; to commend the good among them, and show compassion to the incompetent: — this is the way to treat indulgently men from a distance. To restore families whose line of succession has been broken, and to revive States that have been extinguished; to reduce to order States that are in confusion, and support those which are in peril; to have fixed times for their own reception at court, and the reception of their envoys; to send them away after liberal treatment, and welcome their coming with small contributions: — this is the way to cherish the princes of the States.

1. this is the way for him to encourage his relatives to love him：改译为 “this is the way for him to encourage family affection among his relatives”。

凡为天下国家有九经，所以行之者一也。凡事豫[1]则立，不豫则废。言前定则不跲[2]，事前定则不困，行前定则不疚[3]，道前定则不穷。在下位不获乎上，民不可得而治矣。获乎上有道：不信乎朋友，不获乎上矣。信乎朋友有道：不顺乎亲，不信乎朋友矣。顺乎亲有道：反诸身不诚，不顺乎亲矣。诚身有道：不明乎善，不诚乎身矣。

1. 豫：同“预”，预备。
2. 跲（jiá）：障碍，阻碍。
3. 疚（jiù）：困惑。

15. "All who have the government of the empire with its States and families have the above nine standard rules. And the means by which they are carried into practice is singleness.

16. "In all things success depends on previous preparation, and without such previous preparation there is sure to be failure. If what is to be spoken be previously determined, there will be no stumbling. If affairs be previously determined, there will be no difficulty with them. If one's actions have been previously determined, there will be no sorrow in connection with them. If principles of conduct have been previously determined, the practice of them will be inexhaustible.

17. "When those in inferior situations do not obtain the confidence of the sovereign, they cannot succeed in governing the people. There is a way to obtain the confidence of the sovereign; — if one is not trusted by his friends, he will not get the confidence of his sovereign. There is a way to being trusted by one's friends; — if one is not obedient to his parents, he will not be true to friends. There is a way to being obedient to one's parents; — if one, on turning his thoughts in upon himself, finds a want of sincerity, he will not be obedient to his parents. There is a way to the attainment of sincerity in one's self; — if a man do not understand what is good, he will not attain sincerity in himself.

诚者，天之道也；诚之者，人之道也。诚者不勉而中，不思而得，从容中道，圣人也。诚之者，择善而固执之者也。博学之，审问之，慎思之，明辨之，笃行之。有弗学，学之弗能弗措[1]也；有弗问，问之弗知弗措也；有弗思，思之弗得弗措也；有弗辨，辨之弗明弗措也；有弗行，行之弗笃弗措也。人一能之己百之，人十能之己千之。果能此道矣，虽愚必明，虽柔必强。

1. 弗措：不罢休。

18. "Sincerity is the way of Heaven. The attainment of sincerity is the way of men. He who possesses sincerity hits what is right without an effort, and apprehends without the exercise of thought; —he is the sage who naturally and easily embodies the right way. He who attains to sincerity chooses what is good, and firmly holds it fast.

19. "To this attainment there are requisite the extensive study of what is good, accurate inquiry about it, careful reflection on it, the clear discrimination of it, and the earnest practice of it.

20. "The superior man, while there is anything he has not studied, or while in what he has studied there is anything he cannot understand, will not intermit his labor. While there is anything he has not inquired about, or anything in what he has inquired about which he does not know, he will not intermit his labor. While there is anything which he has not reflected on, or anything in what he has reflected on which he does not apprehend, he will not intermit his labor. While there is anything which he has not discriminated, or his discrimination is not clear, he will not intermit his labor. While there is anything which he has not practiced, or his practice fails in earnestness, he will not intermit his labor. If another man succeed by one effort, he will use a hundred efforts. If another man succeed by ten efforts, he will use a thousand.

21. "Let a man proceed in this way, and, though dull, he will surely become intelligent; though weak, he will surely become strong."

第二十一章

自诚明，谓之性；自明诚，谓之教。诚则明矣，明则诚矣。

When we have intelligence resulting from sincerity, this condition is to be ascribed to nature; when we have sincerity resulting from intelligence, this condition is to be ascribed to instruction. But given the sincerity, and there shall be the intelligence; given the intelligence, and there shall be the sincerity.

第二十二章

唯天下至诚，为能尽其性；能尽其性，则能尽人之性；能尽人之性，则能尽物之性；能尽物之性，则可以赞[1]天地之化育；可以赞天地之化育，则可以与天地参[2]矣。

1. 赞：帮助。
2. 参（cān）：并列。此处指可以和天地并列为三。

It is only he who is possessed of the most complete sincerity that can exist under heaven, who can give its full development to his nature. Able to give its full development to his own nature, he can do the same to the nature of other men. Able to give its full development to the nature of other men, he can give their full development to the natures of animals[1] and things. Able to give their full development to the natures of creatures and things, he can assist the transforming and nourishing powers of Heaven and Earth. Able to assist the transforming and nourishing powers of Heaven and Earth, he may with Heaven and Earth form a ternion[2].

---

1. animals：与下文保持一致，改为“creatures”，因为“creatures and things”比“animals and things”含义更为广泛，包含人之外的所有事物。
2. ternion：三个一套，三合一，三人（事物或思想等）的组合。

第二十三章

其次[1]致曲[2],曲能有诚,诚则形[3],形则著[4],著则明[5],明则动,动则变,变则化,唯天下至诚为能化。

1. 其次：指次于圣人的那类人。
2. 曲：偏，指某个方面。
3. 形：显现。
4. 著：显著。
5. 明：发扬光大。

Next to the above is he who cultivates to the utmost the shoots of goodness in him[1]. From those he can attain to the possession of sincerity. This sincerity becomes apparent. From being apparent, it becomes manifest. From being manifest, it becomes brilliant. Brilliant, it affects others. Affecting others, they are changed by it. Changed by it, they are transformed. It is only he who is possessed of the most complete sincerity that can exist under heaven, who can transform.

1. the shoots of goodness in him："曲"，某一方面。因为只有圣人才可以举其性之全体而尽之，普通人则应该善于发现自己的善端，进而悉推致之，达到其极的境地。所以，"曲"也可译为"a particular goodness"。

第二十四章

至诚之道，可以前知。国家将兴，必有祯祥[1]；国家将亡，必有妖孽；见[2]乎蓍龟[3]，动乎四体。祸福将至：善，必先知之；不善，必先知之。故至诚如神。

1. 祯祥：吉兆。
2. 见：同“现”，呈现。
3. 蓍（shī）龟：古人以蓍草与龟甲占卜凶吉，因此指占卜。

It is characteristic of the most entire sincerity to be able to foreknow. When a nation or family is about to flourish, there are sure to be happy omens; and when it is about to perish, there are sure to be unlucky omens. Such events are seen in the milfoil and tortoise, and affect the movements of the four limbs. When calamity or happiness is about to come, the good shall certainly be foreknown by him, and the evil also. Therefore the individual possessed of the most complete sincerity is like a spirit.

第二十五章

诚者自成也，而道自道[1]也。诚者物之终始，不诚无物。是故君子诚之为贵。诚者非自成己而已也，所以成物也。成己，仁也；成物，知[2]也。性之德也，合外内之道也，故时措之宜也。

1. 道：同“导”。
2. 知：同“智”。

1. Sincerity is that whereby self-completion is effected, and its way is that by which man must direct himself.

2. Sincerity is the end and beginning of things; without sincerity there would be nothing. On this account, the superior man regards the attainment of sincerity as the most excellent thing.

3. The possessor of sincerity does not merely accomplish the self-completion of himself. With this quality he completes other men and things also. The completing himself shows his perfect virtue. The completing other men and things shows his knowledge. Both these are virtues belonging to the nature, and this is the way by which a union is effected of the external and internal. Therefore, whenever he — the entirely sincere man — employs them, — that is, these virtues, their action will be right.

第二十六章

故至诚无息。不息则久，久则征[1]，征则悠远，悠远则博厚，博厚则高明。博厚，所以载[2]物也；高明，所以覆[3]物也；悠久，所以成物也。博厚配地，高明配天，悠久无疆。如此者，不见[4]而章[5]，不动而变，无为而成。天地之道，可一言[6]而尽也：其为物不贰，则其生物不测。天地之道：博也，厚也，高也，明也，悠也，久也。

---

1. 征：显露出来。
2. 载：承载。
3. 覆：覆盖。
4. 见：同“现”。
5. 章：同“彰”。
6. 一言：即“诚”。

1. Hence to entire sincerity there belongs ceaselessness.

2. Not ceasing, it continues long. Continuing long, it evidences itself.

3. Evidencing itself, it reaches far. Reaching far, it becomes large and substantial. Large and substantial, it becomes high and brilliant.

4. Large and substantial; — this is how it contains all things. High and brilliant; — this is how it overspreads all things. Reaching far and continuing long; — this is how it perfects all things.

5. So large and substantial, the individual possessing it is the coequal of Earth. So high and brilliant, it makes him the coequal of Heaven. So far-reaching and long-continuing, it makes him infinite.

6. Such being its nature, without any display, it becomes manifested; without any movement, it produces changes; and without any effort, it accomplishes its ends.

7. The way of Heaven and Earth may be completely declared in one sentence. — They are without any second thought, and so their production of things is inexhaustible.

8. The way of Heaven and Earth is large and substantial, high and brilliant, far-reaching and long-enduring.

今夫天，斯昭昭之多，及其无穷也，日月星辰系焉，万物覆焉。今夫地，一撮土之多，及其广厚，载华岳而不重，振河海而不泄，万物载焉。今夫山，一卷[1]石之多，及其广大，草木生之，禽兽居之，宝藏兴焉。今夫水，一勺之多，及其不测，鼋鼍[2]、蛟龙、鱼鳖生焉，货财殖焉。诗[3]云："维天之命，於[4]穆不已！"盖曰天之所以为天也。"於乎[5]不[6]显！文王之德之纯！"盖曰文王之所以为文也，纯亦不已。

---

1. 卷：通"拳"。
2. 鼋鼍（yuán tuó）：中国神话传说中的动物，一般指巨鳖和扬子鳄。
3. 诗：《诗经·周颂·维天之命》。
4. 於：叹词，同"呜"。
5. 於乎：叹词，同"呜呼"。
6. 不：通"丕"，大。

9. The heaven now before us is only this bright shining spot; but when viewed in its inexhaustible extent, the sun, moon, stars, and constellations of the zodiac, are suspended in it, and all things are overspread by it. The earth before us is but a handful of soil; but when regarded in its breadth and thickness, it sustains mountains like the Hua and the Yue, without feeling their weight, and contains the rivers and seas, without their leaking away. The mountain now before us appears only a stone; but when contemplated in all the vastness of its size, we see how the grass and trees are produced on it, and birds and beasts dwell on it, and precious things which men treasure up are found on it. The water now before us appears but a ladleful; yet extending our view to its unfathomable depths, the largest tortoises, iguanas, iguanodons, dragons, fishes, and turtles, are produced in it, articles of value and sources of wealth abound in it.

10. It is said in the Book of Poetry, "The ordinances of Heaven, how profound are they and unceasing!" The meaning is, that it is thus that Heaven is Heaven. And again, "How illustrious was it, the singleness of the virtue of King Wen!" indicating that it was thus that King Wen was what he was. Singleness likewise is unceasing.

第二十七章

大哉圣人之道！洋洋乎！发育万物，峻[1]极于天。优优[2]大哉！礼仪[3]三百，威仪[4]三千。待其人而后行。故曰苟不至德，至道不凝[5]焉。故君子尊德性而道[6]问学，致广大而尽精微，极高明而道中庸。温故而知新，敦厚以崇礼。是故居上不骄，为下不倍[7]，国有道其言足以兴，国无道其默足以容。诗[8]曰："既明且哲，以保其身"，其此之谓与！

1. 峻：高大。
2. 优优：充足有余。
3. 礼仪：经礼，古代礼节的主要规则。
4. 威仪：曲礼，古代祭享等典礼中的动作规范及待人接物的礼仪。
5. 凝：凝聚。
6. 道：同"导"，由，从。
7. 倍：通"背"，背叛，背弃。
8. 诗：《诗经·大雅·烝民》。

1. How great is the path proper to the Sage!

2. Like overflowing water, it sends forth and nourishes all things, and rises up to the height of heaven.

3. All-complete is its greatness! It embraces the three hundred rules of ceremony, and the three thousand rules of demeanor.

4. It waits for the proper man, and then it is trodden.

5. Hence it is said, "Only by perfect virtue can the perfect path, in all its courses, be made a fact."

6. Therefore, the superior man honors his virtuous nature, and maintains constant inquiry and study, seeking to carry it out to its breadth and greatness, so as to omit none of the more exquisite and minute points which it embraces, and to raise it to its greatest height and brilliancy, so as to pursue the course of the Mean. He cherishes his old knowledge, and is continually acquiring new. He exerts an honest, generous earnestness, in the esteem and practice of all propriety.

7. Thus, when occupying a high situation he is not proud, and in a low situation he is not insubordinate. When the kingdom is well-governed, he is sure by his words to rise; and when it is ill-governed, he is sure by his silence to command forbearance to himself. Is not this what we find in the Book of Poetry, — "Intelligent is he and prudent, and so preserves his person?"

第二十八章

子曰："愚而好自用，贱而好自专，生乎今之世，反[1]古之道。如此者，灾及其身者也。"非天子，不议礼，不制度，不考文。今天下车同轨，书同文，行同伦。虽有其位，苟无其德，不敢作礼乐焉；虽有其德，苟无其位，亦不敢作礼乐焉。子曰："吾说夏礼，杞[2]不足征[3]也；吾学殷礼，有宋[4]存焉；吾学周礼，今用之，吾从周。"

---

1. 反：同"返"。
2. 杞：杞国，自夏代到战国初年的诸侯国，相传大禹的直系后裔居于此。
3. 征：证明。
4. 宋：宋国，周朝的诸侯国，开国国君为商纣王的兄长微子启。

1. The Master said, "Let a man who is ignorant be fond of using his own judgment; let a man without rank be fond of assuming a directing power to himself; let a man who is living in the present age go back to the ways of antiquity; — on the persons of all who act thus calamities will be sure to come."

2. To no one but the emperor does it belong to order ceremonies[1], to fix the measures[2], and to determine the written characters[3].

3. Now over the empire carriages have all wheels of the same size; all writing is with the same characters; and for conduct there are the same rules.

4. One may occupy the throne, but if he have not the proper virtue, he may not dare to make ceremonies or music. One may have the virtue, but if he do not occupy the throne, he may not presume to make ceremonies or music.

5. The Master said, "I may describe the ceremonies of the Xia Dynasty, but Qi cannot sufficiently attest my words. I have learned the ceremonies of the Yin Dynasty, and in Song they still continue. I have learned the ceremonies of Zhou, which are now used, and I follow Zhou."

---

1. to order ceremonies："议礼"指修订礼仪，可改译为"change the rules of propriety"。
2. to fix the measures："制度"指制定宫室车服器具的等级，可改译为"to regulate the standard of customs"。
3. to determine the written characters："考文"指考订文字规范，可改译为"to determine the form and use of the written script"。

第二十九章

王[1]天下有三重[2]焉，其寡过矣乎！上焉者[3]虽善无征[4]，无征不信，不信民弗从；下焉者[5]虽善不尊，不尊不信，不信民弗从。故君子之道：本诸身，征诸庶民，考诸三王[6]而不缪[7]，建诸天地而不悖，质诸鬼神而无疑，百世以俟圣人而不惑。

---

1. 王（wàng）：称王，统治。
2. 三重：三件重要的事情要做，即议定礼仪、制订法度、考订文字。
3. 上焉者：指时王以前，如夏、商的礼制。
4. 征：证明，证验。
5. 下焉者：指圣人在下，如孔子。
6. 三王：指夏、商、周三代君王。
7. 缪：通“谬”，错误。

1. He who attains to the sovereignty of the kingdom[1], having those three important things, shall be able to effect that there shall be few errors under his government.

2. However excellent may have been the regulations of those of former times, they cannot be attested. Not being attested, they cannot command credence, and not being credited, the people would not follow them. However excellent might be the regulations made by one in an inferior situation, he is not in a position to be honored. Unhonored, he cannot command credence, and not being credited, the people would not follow his rules.

3. Therefore the institutions of the ruler are rooted in his own character and conduct, and sufficient attestation of them is given by the masses of the people. He examines them by comparison with those of the three kings, and finds them without mistake. He sets them up before Heaven and Earth, and finds nothing in them contrary to their mode of operation. He presents himself with them before spiritual beings, and no doubts about them arise. He is prepared to wait for the rise of a sage a hundred ages after, and has no misgivings.

---

1. kingdom：“天下”概念大于一个王国，可改译为“empire”，下同。

质诸鬼神而无疑，知天也；百世以俟圣人而不惑，知人也。是故君子动而世为天下道，行而世为天下法，言而世为天下则。远之则有望，近之则不厌。诗[1]曰：“在彼无恶，在此无射[2]；庶几夙夜，以永终誉！”君子未有不如此而蚤[3]有誉于天下者也。

---

1. 诗：《诗经·周颂·振鹭》。
2. 射（yì）：厌弃。
3. 蚤：同“早”。

4. His presenting himself with his institutions before spiritual beings, without any doubts arising about them, shows that he knows Heaven. His being prepared, without any misgivings, to wait for the rise of a sage a hundred ages after, shows that he knows men.

5. Such being the case, the movements of such a ruler, illustrating his institutions, constitute an example to the world for ages. His acts are for ages a law to the kingdom. His words are for ages a lesson to the empire. Those who are far from him look longingly for him; and those who are near him are never wearied with him.

6. It is said in the Book of Poetry, — "Not disliked there, not tired of here, from day to day and night to night, will they perpetuate their praise. " Never has there been a ruler, who did not realize this description, that obtained an early renown throughout the kingdom.

第三十章

仲尼祖述[1]尧、舜，宪章[2]文、武；上律天时，下袭水土。辟[3]如天地之无不持载，无不覆帱[4]，辟如四时之错行，如日月之代明。万物并育而不相害，道并行而不相悖，小德川流，大德敦化，此天地之所以为大也。

---

1. 祖述：遵循前人的行为或学说。
2. 宪章：遵从今人的法则规范。
3. 辟：同“譬”。
4. 覆帱（dào）：遮盖，掩盖。

1. Zhongni handed down the doctrines of Yao and Shun, as if they had been his ancestors, and elegantly displayed the regulations of Wen and Wu, taking them as his model. Above, he harmonized with the times of Heaven, and below, he was conformed to the water and land.

2. He may be compared to Heaven and Earth in their supporting and containing, their overshadowing and curtaining, all things. He may be compared to the four seasons in their alternating progress, and to the sun and moon in their successive shining.

3. All things are nourished together without their injuring one another. The courses of the seasons, and of the sun and moon, are pursued without any collision among them.[1] The smaller energies[2] are like river currents; the greater energies are seen in mighty transformations. It is this which makes Heaven and Earth so great.

---

1. The courses of the seasons ... without any collision among them：改译为 "The courses on which Nature operates run in their own ways without any collision among them"。
2. energies："德" 此处特指天地化育万物的功能，所以 "小德" 可译为 "lesser forces"，"大德" 可译为 "great forces"。

第三十一章

唯天下至圣，为能聪明睿知[1]，足以有临[2]也；宽裕温柔，足以有容也；发强刚毅，足以有执[3]也；齐[4]庄中正，足以有敬也；文理密察，足以有别也。溥博[5]渊泉，而时出之。溥博如天，渊泉如渊。见[6]而民莫不敬，言而民莫不信，行而民莫不说[7]。是以声名洋溢乎中国，施及蛮貊[8]，舟车所至，人力所通，天之所覆，地之所载，日月所照，霜露所队[9]，凡有血气者，莫不尊亲，故曰配天。

1. 知：同“智”。
2. 临：居上而临下，指统治天下。
3. 执：决断。
4. 齐：同“斋”，肃敬。
5. 溥（pǔ）博：周遍广远。
6. 见：同“现”。
7. 说：同“悦”。
8. 蛮貊：古代对南方和北方部族的称呼。
9. 队：同“坠”。

1. It is only he, possessed of all sagely qualities that can exist under heaven, who shows himself quick in apprehension, clear in discernment, of far-reaching intelligence, and all-embracing knowledge, fitted to exercise rule; magnanimous, generous, benign, and mild, fitted to exercise forbearance; impulsive, energetic, firm, and enduring, fitted to maintain a firm hold; self-adjusted, grave, never swerving from the Mean, and correct, fitted to command reverence; accomplished, distinctive, concentrative, and searching, fitted to exercise discrimination.

2. All-embracing is he and vast, deep and active as a fountain, sending forth in their due season his virtues.

3. All-embracing and vast, he is like Heaven. Deep and active as a fountain, he is like the abyss. He is seen, and the people all reverence him; he speaks, and the people all believe him; he acts, and the people all are pleased with him. Therefore his fame overspreads the Middle Kingdom, and extends to all barbarous tribes. Wherever ships and carriages reach; wherever the strength of man penetrates; wherever the heavens overshadow and the earth sustains; wherever the sun and moon shine; wherever frosts and dews fall: — all who have blood and breath unfeignedly honor and love him. Hence it is said: — "He is the equal of Heaven."

第三十二章

唯天下至诚，为能经纶[1]天下之大经，立天下之大本，知天地之化育。夫焉有所倚？肫肫[2]其仁！渊渊[3]其渊！浩浩[4]其天！苟不固聪明圣知[5]达天德者，其孰能知之？

1. 经纶：经、纶皆指纺织前整理丝缕，引申为治理国家大事。
2. 肫（zhūn）肫：诚挚，诚恳。
3. 渊渊：静深的样子。
4. 浩浩：广阔的样子。
5. 知：同“智”。

1. It is only the individual possessed of the most entire sincerity that can exist under Heaven, who can adjust the great invariable relations of mankind, establish the great fundamental virtues of humanity, and know the transforming and nurturing operations of Heaven and Earth; — shall this individual have any being or anything beyond himself on which he depends?

2. Call him man in his ideal, how earnest is he! Call him an abyss, how deep is he! Call him Heaven, how vast is he!

3. Who can know him, but he who is indeed quick in apprehension, clear in discernment, of far-reaching intelligence, and all-embracing knowledge, possessing all heavenly virtue?

第三十三章

诗[1]曰:"衣[2]锦尚䌹[3]",恶其文之著也。故君子之道,暗然而日章[4];小人之道,的然[5]而日亡。君子之道:淡而不厌,简而文,温而理,知远之近,知风之自,知微之显,可与入德矣。诗[6]云:"潜虽伏矣,亦孔[7]之昭!"故君子内省不疚,无恶于志[8]。君子之所不可及者,其唯人之所不见乎。

---

1. 诗:《诗经·卫风·硕人》。原文为"衣锦褧衣","褧"同"䌹"。
2. 衣:穿。
3. 䌹(jiǒng):麻布外衣。
4. 章:同"彰"。
5. 的然:明显的样子。
6. 诗:《诗经·小雅·正月》。
7. 孔:很。
8. 无恶于志:无愧于心。

1. It is said in the Book of Poetry, "Over her embroidered robe she puts[1] a plain single garment," intimating a dislike to the display of the elegance of the former. Just so, it is the way of the superior man to prefer the concealment of his virtue, while it daily becomes more illustrious, and it is the way of the mean man to seek notoriety, while he daily goes more and more to ruin. It is characteristic of the superior man, appearing insipid[2], yet never to produce satiety[3]; while showing a simple negligence, yet to have his accomplishments recognized; while seemingly plain, yet to be discriminating. He knows how what is distant lies in what is near. He knows where the wind proceeds from. He knows how what is minute becomes manifested. Such a one, we may be sure, will enter into virtue.

2. It is said in the Book of Poetry, "Although the fish sink and lie at the bottom, it is still quite clearly seen." Therefore the superior man examines his heart, that there may be nothing wrong there, and that he may have no cause for dissatisfaction with himself. That wherein the superior man cannot be equaled is simply this, — his work which other men cannot see.

---

1. puts：改译为 "wears"。
2. insipid：淡。
3. satiety：饱足。

诗[1]云："相在尔室，尚不愧于屋漏[2]。"故君子不动而敬，不言而信。诗[3]曰："奏假[4]无言，时靡有争。"是故君子不赏而民劝，不怒而民威[5]于铁钺[6]。诗[7]曰："不[8]显惟德！百辟[9]其刑[10]之。"是故君子笃恭而天下平。诗[11]云："予怀明德，不大声以色。"子曰："声色之于以化民，末也。"诗[12]曰："德辅[13]如毛"，毛犹有伦[14]。"上天之载，无声无臭[15]"，至矣！

---

1. 诗：《诗经·大雅·抑》。
2. 屋漏：原指屋子的西北角，此处指戒谨恐惧之心。
3. 诗：《诗经·商颂·烈祖》。
4. 假：同"格"，感格，感通。
5. 威：同"畏"。
6. 铁（fū）钺（yuè）：古代执行军法时用的刀斧。
7. 诗：《诗经·周颂·烈文》。
8. 不：通"丕"，大。
9. 百辟：诸侯百官。
10. 刑：效法。
11. 诗：《诗经·大雅·皇矣》。
12. 诗：《诗经·大雅·蒸民》。
13. 辅（yóu）：古代一种轻便车，引申为轻。
14. 伦：比。
15. 臭（xiù）：气味。

3. It is said in the Book of Poetry, "Looked at in your apartment, be there free from shame as being exposed to the light of Heaven." Therefore, the superior man, even when he is not moving, has a feeling of reverence, and while he speaks not, he has the feeling of truthfulness.

4. It is said in the Book of Poetry, "In silence is the offering presented, and the spirit approached to; there is not the slightest contention." Therefore the superior man does not use rewards, and the people are stimulated to virtue. He does not show anger, and the people are awed more than by hatchets and battle-axes.

5. It is said in the Book of Poetry, "What needs no display is virtue. All the princes imitate it." Therefore, the superior man being sincere and reverential, the whole world is conducted to a state of happy tranquility.

6. It is said in the Book of Poetry, "I regard with pleasure your brilliant virtue, making no great display of itself in sounds and appearances." The Master said, "Among the appliances to transform the people, sounds and appearances are but trivial influences. It is said in another ode, 'His virtue is light as a hair.' Still, a hair will admit of comparison as to its size. 'The doings of the supreme Heaven have neither sound nor smell.' — That is perfect virtue."

《中庸》术语汇编与简释

中庸：doctrine of the mean, the

中，不偏不倚、无过不及。庸，平常。但二者不能截然分开，"庸"是"中"的常然不易状态，"中"要得"常"，二者"一经一纬"，缺一不可。[1]"中庸"二字虽各有其意，实则彼此相通，互为补充，二者兼具才可实现其完整意义。

天：Heaven, heaven, the world

在中国典籍当中，"天"的意蕴非常丰富，可以是抽象符号，代表形而上的本体，即"道"；可以是有形的、自然的天；还可以是具有宗教性、超然的主宰；也可以是人的善心，如同佛家"明心见性"的"心"；也可以是时间和空间的连续，如今天、明天。《中庸》首句的"天"，在汉代是个终极概念，代表"至高无上"，可指元始、天巅、丕大。随着思想的发展，"天"到了宋代指"最高的实体"。根据朱熹注疏，"天以阴阳五行化生万物，气以成形，而理亦赋焉，犹命令也。"他融合了张载和二程的观点。所以，"天"就是自然之理，"天命"就是天理。

性：nature

即理，是个人的和内在的，因"天"赋予人物的"理"不同而"性"各异，但是总体按照儒家"性本善"的观点，是至真、至善、至美的。"性"是可以通"天"的，"性在于心，而原于天"，如《中庸》第二十二章"唯天下至诚，为能尽其性；能尽其性，则能尽人之性；能尽人之性，则能尽物之性；能尽物之性，则可以赞大地之化育；可以赞天地之化育，则可以与天地参矣。"这充分说明儒家思想"体""用"的整体观，人之道与天之道的相通性，所以人才有可能通过修道最终实现"与天地参"的境界。

---

1. 黎靖德：《朱子语类》，北京．中华书局，1986 年版，第 1482—1484 页。

道：**the Path of Duty, Tao, Dao**

原本含义就是“路”，抽象的“道”引申为“人或物所必须遵循的轨道，通称为道。日月星辰所遵循的轨道称为天道，人类生活所遵循的轨道称为人道”。概括起来，“道”在中国哲学中主要含义有：第一，事物的存在都有其变化过程；第二，在事物的变化过程中具有相对不变的规律；第三，事物有其特殊的规律，也有统一的普遍的规律，这普遍的规律就是道；第四，有些思想家把普遍规律抬高到物质世界之上，看作最高的实体、世界的本源，于是成为一个观念的虚构。总之，“道”包含过程与规律的意义，都是客观世界的反映。在《中庸》中，“道”是普遍的规律，是体用结合体，既费且隐，有天道和人道之分。

教：**instruction**

《说文解字》中“教”指“上所施下所效也。从攴从孝。凡教之属皆从教。”“教”就是“效”，是“学”，即学习，循道而学，将后天的不足（那些偏离了至真、至善、至美的地方）改正过来，回归天性，这就是教化。但是在《中庸》里，“教”的指向并不明确，“教”的动作由谁来完成没有明确指出，因此也包括自修研习。包括后面的“自明诚，谓之教”，只说明了结果而没有交代“明”的过程，可以是“自明”，也可以是在他人帮助下的“明”，具有模糊性。在《中庸》中，“教”既言人事又言物事，其含义在首章作为名词，指按照普遍规律加强自身不足之处的过程；在“自明诚，谓之教”中是动词，指“学之”，为求实然之理，即“诚”。

君子：**man of superior virtue, the**

儒家思想传统很少说“什么是”，而说“怎么做”，因此君子的定义可以从其做什么和不做什么来定义。也就是说，是通过规范君子的行为来定义君子的。我们知道，“君子慎其独”“君子中庸”“君子之中庸也，君子而时中”“君子和而不流……中立而不倚……国有道，不变塞焉……国无道，至死不变”“君子遵道而行……君子依乎中庸，遁世不见知而不悔”“君子以人治人，改而止”“君子素其位而行，不愿乎其外……君子无入而不自得焉。在上位不陵下，在下位不援上，正己而不求于人则无怨。上不怨天，下不尤人。故君子居易以俟命，小人行险以徼幸”“射有似乎君子，失诸正鹄，反求诸其身”“君子诚之为贵”“君子尊德性而道问学，致广大而尽精微，极高明而道中庸。温故而知新，敦厚以崇礼。是故居上不骄，为下不倍，国有道其言足以兴，国无道其默足以容”“君子动而世为天下道，行而世为天下法，言而世为天下则。远之则有望，近之则不厌”“君子之道，暗然而日章……淡而不厌，简而文，温而理，知远之近，知风之自，知微之显，可与入德矣”“君子内省不疚，无恶于志”“君子不动而敬，不言而信”“君子笃恭而天下平”。

小人：the mean man

与“君子”定义方式相同，“小人”的定义也是通过其行为方式来确定的。“小人反中庸”“小人之（反）中庸也，小人而无忌惮也”“小人行险以徼幸”“小人之道，的然而日亡”。

慎独：being watchful over himself, when he is alone

独者，人所不知而己所独知之地也。《中庸》出现“慎独”是在“莫见乎隐，莫显乎微，故君子慎其独也”一句中，说的是在幽暗之中，细微之事，虽然还没有迹象，但自己已经感受到变化，别人虽然不知但自己已经知晓，相比天下之事，这再明显不过了。所以，君子常常戒惧于此，非常谨慎，要做到将欲望抑制在萌芽状态，不能任其在隐微中滋长，以至于偏离正道。“慎独”在《大学》中接连出现过两次，讲的是要自我修养的人需要知道为善，以便去除邪恶，那就要真正付出努力，要禁止自欺欺人。所以，君子“慎独”，必须对其内心的变化非常谨慎。

中和：states of equilibrium and harmony, the

喜、怒、哀、乐等情感，在没有表现出来之前，处于平和状态，是本性所在，无所偏倚，称之为中；表现出来而有所节制，是情感的正常展现，无所乖戾，称之为和。中是根本，是天命之性，天下之理皆由此出，是道的本体。达道的人就是循性而为之人。性情之德，用以明道，不可或缺。这要以戒惧来约束，以至于至静之中，不会偏倚，从而守住不失，等到达到了“中”的最高境界，天地就会各就其位。从慎独开始，进而明察秋毫，以至于在处理事务时，不会有差谬，一切适然，等到达到“和”的最高境界，万物就会繁育生长，“和”道之用。这也就是说，天地万物与本我是一体，本我之心正，天地之心就正，本我之气顺，天地之气就顺。所以，做学问的功夫、圣人所能之事，都概莫能外，修道的教化功能也包含其中。

仁：benevolence

“仁”的意义比较宽泛，包容面广。朱熹认为，“仁者，天地生物之心，而人得以生者，所谓元者善之长也”“人，指人身而言。具此生理，自然便有恻怛慈爱之意，深体会之可见。”可见，“仁”是由人的生理所定，是天性使然，即孟子的性善之说。朱熹所说的“爱之理，心之德”即是“仁”，是爱的原则和心的本质。“仁”是儒家思想的最高道德原则，其黄金法则为“施诸己而不愿，亦勿施于人”，正面说法是“己欲立而立人，己欲达而达人”（《论语·雍也》）。“仁”的最高表现，也是基本要求，是“亲亲”，由内推外。“仁”成为处理人际关系的表现，但首先要从自身、从亲近的人出发。“为政在人，取人以身，修身以道，修道以仁”，人是为政的关键，但首先要修身，修身就要合乎道，以仁行事就可达道。

义：justice, righteousness

“义”是儒家思想“四端”仁义礼智的核心思想之一。如上所述，“仁”体现人与人之间相亲相爱的关系，是儒家思想的最高道德原则，“义”则是儒家思想泛指的道德原则，体现在处理人际关系时的恰当与合乎规律。按照《大学》的八目（格物、致知、诚意、正心、修身、齐家、治国、平天下），在治理国家时能够让有能力之人各得其所、尽其才、有用武之地，就达到了“义”的最高层次，即“义者，宜也，尊贤为大”的核心内涵。“义”突出的是“宜”，合乎规律，是常然之道，是讲道义的表现。孟子所说“羞恶之心，义也”就是“义”的道德意识含义，而“理也，义也”是推己及人，将个体性情推及、提升到普遍意义的性情，具有法则、准则的含义。

礼：rule, ceremony, principle of propriety

“礼”是亲疏贵贱相接之体，合乎礼法，是对自然（鬼神乃阴阳合散所为，为物之体，物所不能遗）和社会规律（孝为先导，上至帝王，下至平民，推己及人，概莫能外）的敬畏，是对和谐有序存在的维护。“亲亲之杀，尊贤之等，礼所生也”中的“杀”和“等”都表示“等级”，对亲人要体现出亲疏，对有能力之人要让其适得其所，发挥自己的作用，所以划分等级也是“礼”。治理国家所需的“九经”充分体现了从提升自身品格做起应该遵循的规范，这也是处理好人际关系应遵循的“礼”。“仁”是从自身做起建立良好人际关系的起点，也是最高道德要求，“义”从宏观上告诉人们处理人际关系的原则，而“礼”则指明处理人际关系时的具体做法，表现为具体的习俗、礼节、仪式，如祭祀之礼、宗庙之礼，有宏观之礼（礼仪，经礼也），有微观之礼（威仪，曲礼也）。“礼”也是对社会关系和社会伦理的整套规范表达，如夏礼、殷礼、周礼。由于“仁”是儒家思想道德的最高要求，在以“礼”为基础的人际关系中，重视对推己及人、礼让他人、礼贵他人等品质的强调，体现了儒家思想在行为和精神上的高度统一。总体来说，“礼”体现的是一种道德伦理观念，具有非制度化特征，不具有法律约束力。

诚：sincerity, integrity, honesty, being true to oneself

真实无妄，人事之当然。诚具有多重意涵，天诚（诚者）和人诚（诚之者）是不同的。诚具有道德形上学意义，是自我实现在本体论上的自决与自我修养在生存论上的必要，要求人的内在道德性在具体的日常事务中得到实现，这既是对己也是对天的义务，其核心是坚持教育的中心地位。诚既是存在状态也是生成过程，是一种创造形式，是天地化育过程得以出现的原动力。诚是原初本真状态的实在，是天人合一的终极基础，是创造性转化的伟大源泉。

忠恕：principle of reciprocity, the

尽己之心为忠，推己及人为恕。常用“施诸己而不愿，亦勿施于人”来表达忠恕之道，即以己之心度人之心，己之所不欲，则勿以施之于人，与张载所说的“以爱己之心爱人则尽仁”有异曲同工之妙。

曾子　子思
The Great Learning & The Doctrine of the Mean

图书在版编目（CIP）数据

大学·中庸 = The Great Learning & The Doctrine of the Mean：汉英对照 /（春秋）曾子，（春秋）子思著；（英）理雅各（James Legge）译；杨文地注释. —上海：上海译文出版社，2021.11
（世界学术经典系列）
ISBN 978-7-5327-8705-0

Ⅰ.①大… Ⅱ.①曾… ②子… ③理… ④杨… Ⅲ.①儒家 ②《大学》—注释—汉、英 ③《中庸》—注释—汉、英 Ⅳ.①B222.12

中国版本图书馆CIP数据核字（2021）第161008号

大学·中庸（汉英对照版）
曾子　子思　著［英］理雅各　译　杨文地　导读　注释
责任编辑 / 陆亚平　装帧设计 / 张志全工作室

上海译文出版社有限公司出版、发行
网址：www.yiwen.com.cn
200001　上海福建中路193号
江阴市机关印刷服务有限公司印刷

开本 890×1240　1/32　印张 5.75　插页 6　字数 139,000
2022年1月第1版　2022年1月第1次印刷
印数：0,001–2,000册

ISBN 978-7-5327-8705-0/B·507
定价：75.00元

World Academic Classics
世界学术经典·英文版

Marxism
马克思主义

The Communist Manifesto (Marx & Engels)
共产党宣言（马克思、恩格斯）

Chinese Classics
中国经典

论语（汉英对照）
Confucius' Analects

道德经（汉英对照）
Dao De Jing

孟子（汉英对照）
Mencius

庄子（汉英对照）
Zhuangzi

孙子兵法（汉英对照）
Sun Tzu on the Art of War

大学·中庸（汉英对照）
The Great Learning & The Doctrine of the Mean

Philosophy
哲　学

Republic (Plato)
理想国（柏拉图）

Metaphysics (Aristotle)
形而上学（亚里士多德）

Meditations on First Philosophy (René Descartes)
第一哲学沉思录（笛卡尔）

A Discourse on Method (René Descartes)
方法论（笛卡尔）

Pascal's Pensées (Blaise Pascal)
思想录（帕斯卡尔）

A Treatise of Human Nature (David Hume)
人性论（休谟）

Critique of Pure Reason (Kant)
纯粹理性批判（康德）

Critique of Judgement (Kant)
判断力批判（康德）

The Phenomenology of Mind (Hegel)
精神现象学（黑格尔）

The Logic of Hegel (Hegel)
小逻辑（黑格尔）

The World as Will and Representation (Schopenhauer)
作为意志与表象的世界（叔本华）

Thus Spake Zarathustra (Nietzsche)
查拉图斯特拉如是说（尼采）

Either / Or (Kierkegaard)
非此即彼（克尔凯郭尔）

Ideas: General Introduction to Pure Phenomenology (Husserl)
纯粹现象学导论（胡塞尔）

On First Philosophy (Husserl)
论第一哲学（胡塞尔）

Tractatus Logico-Philosophicus (Wittgenstein)
逻辑哲学论（维特根斯坦）

Philosophical Investigations (Wittgenstein)
哲学研究（维特根斯坦）

Pragmatism (William James)
实用主义（威廉·詹姆斯）

Reconstruction in Philosophy (John Dewey)
哲学的改造（杜威）

Time and Free Will (Henri Bergson)
时间与自由意志（柏格森）

A Discourse on the Positive Spirit (Auguste Comte)
论实证精神（孔德）

Novum Organum (Francis Bacon)
新工具（培根）

Ethics
伦理学

The Nicomachean Ethics of Aristotle (Aristotle)
尼各马可伦理学（亚里士多德）

The Theory of Moral Sentiments (Adam Smith)
道德情操论（亚当·斯密）

A Discourse on Inequality (Rousseau)
论人类不平等的起源与基础（卢梭）

Critique of Practical Reason (Kant)
实践理性批判（康德）

Utilitarianism (Mill)
功利主义（密尔）

Principia Ethica (Moore)
伦理学原理（摩尔）

Religion
宗教学

Confessions (St. Augustine)
忏悔录（圣·奥古斯丁）

Basic Writings of Saint Thomas Aquinas (Thomas Aquinas)
圣托马斯基本著作（阿奎那）

Basic Theological Writings (Martin Luther)
路德基本著作选（马丁·路德）

The Courage to Be (Paul Tillich)
存在的勇气（蒂利希）

The Essence of Christianity (Ludwig Feuerbach)
基督教的本质（费尔巴哈）

Politics
政治学

The Politics of Aristotle (Aristotle)
政治学（亚里士多德）

The Prince (Machiavelli)
君主论（马基雅维利）

The Social Contract (Rousseau)
社会契约论（卢梭）

Leviathan (Thomas Hobbes)
利维坦（霍布斯）

Two Treatises of Government (John Locke)
政府论（洛克）

The Spirit of the Laws (Montesquieu)
论法的精神（孟德斯鸠）

Democracy in America (Tocqueville)
论美国民主（托克维尔）

Considerations on Representative Government (Mill)
代议制政府（密尔）

The Federalist Papers (Hamilton)
联邦党人文集（汉密尔顿）

The Ancien Régime and the Revolution (Tocqueville)
旧制度与大革命（托克维尔）

Utopia (Thomas More)
乌托邦（莫尔）

On Liberty (Mill)
论自由（密尔）

Reflections on the Revolution in France (Edmund Burke)
评法国革命（伯克）

The Will to Power (Nietzsche)
权力意志（尼采）

On War (Carl von Clausewitz)
战争论（克劳塞维茨）

Mutual Aid: A Factor of Evolution (Kropotkin)
互助论（克鲁泡特金）

Economics
经济学

The Economics of Welfare (Pigou)
福利经济学（庇古）

Principles of Economics (Alfred Marshall)
经济学原理（马歇尔）

The General Theory of Employment, Interest and Money (Keynes)
就业、利息与货币通论（凯恩斯）

The Theory of Economic Development (Schumpeter)
经济发展理论（熊彼特）

An Inquiry into the Nature and Causes of the Wealth of Nations (Adam Smith)
国民财富的性质和原因的研究（亚当·斯密）

Capitalism, Socialism and Democracy (Schumpeter)
资本主义、社会主义与民主（熊彼特）

An Essay on Population (Thomas Robert Malthus)
人口原理（马尔萨斯）

The Principles of Scientific Management (Frederick Winslow Taylor)
科学管理原理（泰勒）

Sociology
社会学

Suicide: A Study in Sociology (Durkheim)
自杀：社会学研究（迪尔凯姆）

The Protestant Ethic and the Spirit of Capitalism (Max Weber)
新教伦理与资本主义精神（韦伯）

The Philosophy of Money (Georg Simmel)
货币哲学（西美尔）

A Treatise on General Sociology (Vilfredo Pareto)
社会学总论（帕累托）

Ideology and Utopia (Mannheim)
意识形态与乌托邦（曼海姆）

First Principles (Herbert Spencer)
基本原理（斯宾塞）

The Theory of the Leisure Class (Thorstein B. Veblen)
论闲逸阶级（凡勃伦）

Anthropology
人类学

The Golden Bough (James George Frazer)
金枝（詹姆斯·乔治·弗雷泽）

Argonauts of the Western Pacific (Malinowski)
西太平洋的航海者（马林诺夫斯基）

Structure and Function in Primitive Society (Radcliffe-Brown)
原始社会的结构和功能（拉德克利夫–布朗）

Race, Language and Culture (Franz Boas)
种族、语言与文化（弗朗茨·博厄斯）

The Savage Mind (Claude Lévi-Strauss)
野性思维（克劳德·列维–斯特劳斯）

Psychology
心理学

The Principles of Psychology (William James)
心理学原理（威廉·詹姆斯）

Principles of Physiological Psychology (Wundt)
生理心理学原理（冯特）

The Interpretation of Dreams (Sigmund Freud)
梦的解析（弗洛伊德）

The Archetypes and the Collective Unconscious (Jung)
原型与集体无意识（荣格）

Law
法　学

Ancient Law (Maine)
古代法（梅因）

English Law and the Renaissance (Maitland)
英国法律与文艺复兴（梅特兰）

Lectures on Jurisprudence (Austin)
法理学演讲录（奥斯丁）

Fundamental Principles of the Sociology of Law (Ehrlich)
法律社会学基本原理（埃利希）

History
历史学

The Histories (Herodotus)
历史（希罗多德）

The Peloponnesian War (Thucydides)
伯罗奔尼撒战争史（修昔底德）

The Annals of Imperial Rome (Tacitus)
编年史（塔西佗）

The City of God (St. Augustine)
上帝之城（圣·奥古斯丁）

On Heroes, Hero Worship, and the Heroic in History (Thomas Carlyle)
论历史上的英雄、英雄崇拜和英雄业绩（卡莱尔）

The Idea of History (Collingwood)
历史的观念（科林伍德）

History of Civilization in Europe (Francois Guizot)
欧洲文明史（基佐）

The Influence of Sea Power (Alfred T. Mahan)
海权对历史的影响（马汉）

Theory & History of Historiography (Benedetto Croce)
史学理论与史学史（克罗齐）

A Short Account of the Destruction of the Indies (Bartolomé de Las Cases)
西印度毁灭述略（卡萨斯）

Literary Theory and Aesthetics
文学理论与美学

On the Art of Poetry (Aristotle)
诗学（亚里士多德）

On the Art of Poetry (Horace)
诗艺（贺拉斯）

On the Sublime (Longinus)
论崇高（朗吉努斯）

Theory of Aesthetic / History of Aesthetic (Benedetto Croce)
美学理论 / 美学史（克罗齐）

Hegel's Aesthetics Lectures on Fine Art (Hegel)
黑格尔美学讲演录（黑格尔）

The Birth of Tragedy (Friedrich Nietzsche)
悲剧的诞生（尼采）

Linguistics
语言学

Course in General Linguistics (Saussure)
普通语言学教程（索绪尔）

On Language (Wilhelm von Humboldt)
论语言（威廉·冯·洪堡特）

Scientific Philosophy
自然科学哲学

On the Origin of Species (Charles Darwin)
物种起源（查尔斯·达尔文）

Mathematical Principles of Natural Philosophy and Its System of the World (Issac Newton)
自然哲学的数学原理（牛顿）

Natural History (Pliny the Elder)
自然史（老普林尼）